BRAIN TATTOOS

Creating Unique Brands That
Stick in Your Customers' Minds

Karen Post

Foreword by Jeffery H. Gitomer

Afterword by Michael Tchong

AMACOM AMERICAN MANAGEMENT ASSOCIATION
NEW YORK • ATLANTA • BRUSSELS • CHICAGO • MEXICO CITY
SAN FRANCISCO • SHANGHAI • TOKYO • TORONTO • WASHINGTON, D.C.

This publication is designed to provide accurate and authoritative information in regard to the subject matter covered. It is sold with the understanding that the publisher is not engaged in rendering legal, accounting, or other professional service. If legal advice or other expert assistance is required, the services of a competent professional person should be sought.

Library of Congress Cataloging-in-Publication Data

Post, Karen.
    Brain tattoos : creating unique brands that stick in your customers' minds / Karen Post ; foreword by Jeffery H. Gitomer ; afterword by Michael Tchong.
        p.   cm.
    Includes bibliographical references and index.
    ISBN 0–8144–7234–6
    1. Brand name products.   2. Brand name products—Marketing.   I. Title.
HD69.B7P64 2005
658.8'27—dc22

                                                                    2004014340

Printing number

10   9   8   7   6   5   4   3   2

Dedicated to my dear Jody
for his unconditional support and sense of humor

and to my awesome mom and sister, Cathy,
for without their encouragement and acceptance of my
overstimulated right brain, this journey would not have been possible.

In memory of my dad, Norm Post,
whose resilient spirit and positive outlook lives in me every day.

Contents

Chapter 4: Brand Warriors: Qualities of Great Brand Builders   47

Chapter 5: Branding Basics: How to Construct Your Tattoo Plan   64

Chapter 6: Brand Naming: Art, Skill, and Luck   74

Chapter 7: Four Engines of Brand Development   83

Chapter 8: The Fifth Engine: Eleven Tattoo Tactics That Speak Loudly Even When You Whisper   111

Chapter 9: Internal Branding: Breathing the Brand into Your Organization

Chapter 10: Before You Brand, Protect Your Assets

Epilogue: Top-Ten Tattoo Taboos

Foreword

Jeffrey H. Gitomer
Brand "X"—Exposure to get known, Execution for Results . . .

Jeffrey Gitomer is author of *The Sales Bible; Customer Satisfaction Is Worthless, Customer Loyalty Is Priceless; The Patterson Principles of Selling;* and *The Little Red Book of Selling.*

What's your brand?

Not just your company brand and your product brand—I'm also talking about your *personal* brand. All are critical to success.

In sales, prospects buy the salesperson *first*. If they buy brand-you, then they may buy the brand you're selling. How do you get a brand? How do you create a brand? Easy answer—study this book.

Branding is not complicated, unless you take a course in it. Then it's scary as hell. Branding is a combination of instinct, insight, ideas, and the drive to convert your marketing into your brand.

I have a brand. Or should I say: *I AM the brand.* I have taken my name, "Gitomer" and "Jeffrey Gitomer," and turned it into my brand. My column has been in the *Charlotte Business Journal* every week for eleven years. It's now in eighty-five markets. My Web site is my name: gitomer.com. My company is my name: Buy Gitomer. And everything I do has my name on it. (I even registered the URLs for the misspellings of my name.)

I'd love to tell you that I studied branding from the masters, but I did not. My branding came about by accident. I didn't realize I was building one until I had one. I thought branding was something that only big companies did. Jell-O, Kleenex, Lexus, Nordstrom—those are brands. Brand Gitomer? Well, admittedly it's a lesser brand, but it's built my niche—and that's all that matters to me.

How are you building yours? Here's the answer you're looking for:

Karen Post is the Branding Diva. And for good reason. She's been at branding for over twenty years. She's passionate, creative, and fearless. You will get her brand in this book.

It's not just about the big brand picture. It's about brand action, and the actions you need to take to build yours. You've all heard of hands-on action—this book is brands-on action. The power of your brand is determined by others. But the actions you take can influence them to build it.

Karen will show you a new way—a result of your total branding and marketing outreach—to make your phone ring with qualified prospects, convert them to sales, and add value to your operation.

It's something you can't place an exact value on or buy, but it's the difference between image and no image, the difference between recognition and anonymity, the difference between sale and no sale. And the difference between having to sell and people wanting to buy.

If you merely read this book, you're doing yourself a disservice—you need to study it and put the ideas into action. The result of these actions will be a brand-new you.

Acknowledgments

Although I have not borne a child, I feel the birthing of this book was a similar experience. It took about nine months. There were days of great joy and others of monumental fear. I gained a little weight (looking forward to losing that). It was emotional and an experience I will not soon forget. But most of all, I am grateful and could not have done it alone. I had an incredible team of support and inspiration. To the new friends I met while writing the book, my agent, my business advisers, all the folks at AMACOM, my branding peers, my clients, my family, and my friends—thank you for everything. *Brain Tattoos* would not have been born without your contributions.

All the AMACOM Folks
William Abrams
Wendy Aimes Rowe
John Ambrose
Brad Augsburger
Dave Balter
Traci Bild
Jim Blasingame
Karen Brogno
Dr. Neal Burns
Joe Calloway
John Carter
Larry Chase

Kristen Friend
Jeffrey Gitomer
David Glickman
Michael Glickman
Marc Gobé
Seth Godin
Allan Gorman
Jim Gossen
Jill Griffin
Alexis Gutzman
Tom Henken
Naseem Javed
Lynn Johnson

Carole McClendon
Sarah McNeill
Stephanie Melnick
Mitch Meyerson
Michael Michalko
Robert P. Miles
Marty Neumeier
Tommy O'Neal
Jim Phillips
Maxie Post
Millie Post
Donna Reiter
Juan Romero

Ellen Coleman
Howard Davis
Anne Dejoie
Pat Dominquez
Brian Emerson
Sam Ewen
Patti Eyres
Susan Farb Morris
Dwayne Flinchum
Peter Francese

Cathy Jury
Willard Jackson
JJ Jury
Krissy Jury
Ellen Kadin
Judy King
Jody Larriviere
Sue Mack
James J. Mammarella
Diana Marshall

Dan Roselli
Heath Row
Abram Sauer
Seth M. Siegel
Doug Stevenson
John Taylor
Michael Tchong
Jack Trout
Micheal Weissenfluh

Introduction

Brands are a vital part of our economy, our culture, and our society. Buyers in every category are affected by this psychological deluge. Some claim they are a part of the anti-brand crowd. They prefer private-label products by someone they trust, like Sears or Wal-Mart. Last time I looked, Sears and Wal-Mart were mighty brand forces, if not leading brand names.

Maybe, to consumers, brands are not equally important in all categories. Some of us may be content with generic laundry detergent but would not consider a generic haircare product. In some cases, we may not be completely conscious of brands and simply take them for granted. I have no doubt, however, that if I searched the homes of even hardcore anti-brand buyers, I would find branded goods that they selected over a competing product or service.

The word *brand* has many definitions from a variety of respected resources. I believe the brand is a mental imprint that is earned and belongs to a product, service, organization, individual, and/or event. It's a story embedded in the mind of the market. It's the sum of all tangible and intangible characteristics of that entity. A brand is what an audience thinks and feels when it hears a name or sees a sign, a product, and/or a place of activity. It's what customers expect when they select an offering over a competing one.

Many people associate a branded anything with a nationally exposed, big company or product commanding a premium price, compared to an unbranded or private-label offering. While a few years ago, I would have agreed in theory, today the world of branding and branded goods has a much different face. Private-label goods now have brand value due to their powerful retail parents—Wal-Mart and Target, for example. Branding done right can significantly benefit any size company or offering that follows the universal principles of building and breathing a brand.

The concept of branding can be confusing. Today's marketplace pumps out trillions of messages every second. The average consumer is assaulted by more than 3,500 brand messages every day. The marketplace is noisy, crowded, cluttered, and very perplexing. Competition is rampant, and even brands that are not in a company's market or category can make a weak brand fade into obscurity.

To achieve successful branding sometimes requires a radical shift in thinking by its leadership. Branding is not merely the logo, some catchy tagline, or the creative pastime for the marketing department. Branding is a way of life. Branding is the heart and soul of an offering. It should be woven into every important decision and resonate through every point of contact within a market's span.

I asked veteran marketing expert John Carter, who has spent the last four decades playing in the ocean of business with some of the largest and most powerful branding agencies in the world, for his take on branding. John served as executive creative director for both Ogilvy & Mather and DMB&B, both considered the world's best ad agencies. He suggested that branding is a way to keep critical thinking from happening when your best customers are in the process of making a purchase. "It's why America has become one of the most dumbed-down first-world societies on the planet. Branding is habit, marketing voodoo. Business wants minds that are addicted to its propaganda. Since humans are such fickle critters, it is often not worth what it takes to get them into a hypnotized, semi-zombie state of buying. Many nonpublic, smaller companies don't stay in existence long enough or have the skill sets necessary to get much of a branding payoff. They are more in the pirate trade: Disrupt the established brands and move on to the next sluggish Spanish galleon which has a turning circle at least the size of an average, bloated corporate bureaucracy.

"So the main thing the smart business needs to know is how to bust a well-branded company long enough to take some loot. For this, a guerrilla marketing mind-set comes in handy. In some cases, a raider approach is actually hindered when resources are spent for branding over too long a time. It means you've started trying to play the top dog's game, and that is never wise when you are a pirate. It generally leads to capture, extermination, or conversion to a despicable new corporate faith unworthy of the free, untamed life of a buccaneer."

Branding today needs to get down to business. Go beyond marketing, touch every point of the market, enlist all warriors, and embrace a "whatever it takes" attitude.

Branding has a fearless new face. Roll up your sleeves. Put on your thick skin. It's time for *Brain Tattoos*. This approach will take any size business through the deep and dangerous waters of tough economies, capricious customers, and ever-changing times.

What a Brain Tattoo Can Do for You

A Brain Tattoo is a stronger brand than the norm, rich with promise, bold with purpose, distinct and prominently inked onto your buyer's cranium.

With this book I hope to open your eyes to new, exciting branding possibilities. It is intended to stimulate creative cells that may be napping and give all business leaders a real-world, step-by-step formula to build a more profitable company, sell more product, and attract and keep the most talented employees. Most of all, it will allow you to enjoy the fruits of your hard work. The size of your enterprise does not matter; it is your decision to build, protect, and leverage your Brain Tattoo as an important asset in your business model that counts.

If you are looking for scientific theory and rooms full of quantified research, this book is not for you. I respect a balance of those disciplines in the brand development and decision-making process. However, these pages bring firsthand experiences from the real-world business trenches. After all, many of the greatest brands ever "just did it" while others were researching away and missed the boat. There is also insight "From the Brain Trust," a diverse group of branding and business professionals.

A Brain Tattoo is reality branding—straight from a practitioner's war chest and topped off with smart and successful branding examples. A Brain Tattoo can deliver:

> ➤ **Significant Value.** We're talking balance sheet value! How do a few extra million dollars in your pocket sound? An increase

in your stock price? A Brand Tattoo can build new assets in your organization.

> **Lifetime Customer Loyalty.** We all know that keeping loyal customers is worth more and costs a lot less than getting new ones.
> **Higher Selling Prices, Thus Returning Greater Margins.** Many buyers will pay 6 percent to 12 percent more for branded goods and services.
> **The Ability to Retain Superstar Employees.** Companies with strong brands are more likely to attract and keep loyal, superstar team players.

Whether you are selling a product to consumers or a service to the business-to-business market, do the math—branding works. More than likely you are already doing some stuff. You just need to be doing the right stuff that tells your brand story.

What's more, branding can be a total blast. Have some fun, do something new and bold, enlist all of your employees to be champions of the brand. Energize your corporate culture with brand buzz. Haven't you heard that happy stakeholders who enjoy and take pride in their organization are the foundation for a successful operation?

How to Get the Most from *Brain Tattoos*

This book is built on simple, practical processes, creative possibilities, and behavioral attitudes. All sections must be embraced to achieve brand brilliance.

If you prefer fast brain food, at the end of every chapter you have the highly popular Five-Second Brand Bites. Grab a cup of whatever you drink, open your mind, and start a new journey to the land of Brain Tattoos, where margins are mightier, loyalty lasts, and businesses bloom.

Read the book in its entirety, then return to audit your current branding efforts or opportunities so you can create and work from a plan. Enlist your support team and advisers, and trust your instinct. Revisit the book regularly and use the brand bites as refresher tools.

Chapter 1 explores in-depth the essence of the brand, branding opportunities, and strategies for brand growth. It also introduces super Brain Tattoo examples in a variety of consumer and business-to-business sectors.

Chapter 2 exposes the hard truth about your brand. Is it healthy or on a sinking ship? The tattoo tests will help you quickly diagnose the situation.

Chapter 3 is about you and achieving your goals with the help of a personal brand. This chapter provides examples, tools, and tactics to help you stand out in your professional space.

Chapter 4 is about mental mindfulness of great brand leaders. The elite group of leaders who build brand legacies have some characteristics in common. Brain Tattoos are the product of this behavior and leadership attitude.

Chapter 5 walks you through the vital information-gathering and environment analysis process, and then breaks the brand essence into manageable cells for creating a lasting brand story.

Chapter 6 introduces the crucial naming process. A great brand name can dramatically impact the future of a brand's life. A weak name can make the journey long and miserable.

All Brain Tattoos are equipped with five engines for power and stamina. Chapter 7 discusses the strategic components and how to make sure they are part of your brand. Chapter 8 completes the winning brand model with the fifth engine, explaining eleven tattoo tactics for memorial and efficient communication.

Chapter 9 addresses how a brand becomes the backbone of an organization's culture and serves as a magnet for attracting the best human talent. Here you will learn how to build an assertive strong army of brand ambassadors.

Chapter 10 speaks to protecting your brand's intellectual properties. It's a shame to create a home-run idea and then discover that the asset legally belongs to someone else.

In addition to my take on branding, there are boatloads of excellent books and resources on the subject. You'll find a thorough list under Resources at the end of the book. Explore them carefully, and apply what works for your particular situation. Remember, one branding boot does not fit all.

Branding has been part of my professional life for more than twenty years. I began as a visual merchandiser in Dallas, Texas, in the early 1980s. After one year in college, I terminated my formal education for the more challenging entrepreneurial track. Making minimum wage and doing whatever no one else wanted to do, I knew I was buying precious work experience while I waited for my true career calling.

That came from a chance encounter at the Magnolia Bar & Grill. After a brief conversation, while waiting for a table, with the owner of this new restaurant, I smelled an opportunity. We exchanged cards, and a business meeting was set up. A few days later we hooked up. I came prepared with my massive list of questions to understand fully his business and goals. I listened, took extensive notes, and committed to delivering a proposal within a week.

Now the reality of the situation hit me. He needed a proposal and plan to take this business from "new and unknown" to "on the map and branded." Then my entrepreneurialism kicked in and I organized my goals, developed simple strategies, created a plan of action, and scheduled a presentation with the owner.

To my amazement, the proposal was solid and the presentation went extremely well. I got the job! True, I was paid only in food and drink, but it was a job. Plan in hand, we kicked off a grassroots, mixed-media campaign with a strong focus on public relations and event marketing. By the spring of 1982, after a string of successful initiatives, the holding corporation of The Magnolia Bar & Grill, Louisiana Fine Foods Company Inc., which also owned several other restaurant properties and a wholesale food supply and catering company, officially engaged me as its marketing/communications agency of record.

Granted, the terms used to describe marketing and branding activities have evolved over the years, but the root of this success remains the same. In business you find a need and fill it. Be authentic, have a unique dimension, connect through emotions, confirm through logic, consistently communicate your story, deliver on your promise, and then go to the bank and play lots of tennis. I believe marketing is the working process, and your brand is the result.

Soon thereafter, I cofounded a public relations agency with ultimate communications professional Susan Farb Morris and later bought her out and built two new firms handling consumer and business-to-business marketing and litigation communications. I have worked with a slew of great organizations and leaders and their brands. From for-profits to nonprofits, consumer, B2B, and technology firms, small emerging start-ups to Fortune 500 companies, along with professional athletes and elected officials, I've seen a lot: Branding is in my blood. It's my goal to help you increase your healthy cell count and build your business with bold, compelling, and lasting Brain Tattoos.

chapter 1

Your Brand: How to Create an Indelible Mental Mark

It blows my mind to think how many professionals and business-people don't really understand commercial branding. They still think it's all about the cows—and a sizzling-hot iron used to distinguish cattle. While there is some similarity to that practice, commercial branding spans far beyond the pasture and affects all of us.

Cattlemen used to brand with a burned-on visual symbol to differentiate one rancher's herd from another, thus protecting a valuable asset. Their focus was on the butt, and the process involved some degree of pain. Commercial branding, on the other hand, directs its efforts to the brain and, if managed properly, can deliver a high degree of reward and pleasure.

Some say the term *brand name* originated among American distillers, who branded their names and emblems on their kegs before shipment. Some even say President Lincoln, when informed that General Grant drank whiskey while leading his troops, reportedly replied, "Find out the name of the brand so I can give it to my other generals."

Today in business, the term *branding* has a much grander role. Brands have an impact on cultures, create lasting memories, reduce mental anxiety, and serve as needed fuel for thriving economies everywhere. A commercial brand is an emotional relationship between the buying market and a marketed product or service—a bond of loyalty, a connection of relevance and earned trust.

A brand, or what I refer to as a Brain Tattoo™, is a psychological impression of value-based emotions, lodged in the mind of a buyer or prospect. Just like a traditional ink printed on some body part, a Brain

Tattoo is put there by choice, because it has some very personal and intimate value, and it can be removed at any time.

A brand is not just a logo, a catchy tagline, or a clever ad. Rather, it is *the sum* of all a company or offering does through every point of contact with and into its market. From customer service to a Web presence, a brand is what sticks to a buyer's brain—the mental mark—and it is a crucial factor in the purchasing decision.

FROM THE BRAIN TRUST

What Is Your Definition of a Brand?

"Who you are, what you promise, and your ability and willingness to deliver on that promise."
—JOE CALLOWAY, *author of* Becoming a Category of One: How Extraordinary Companies Transcend Commodity and Defy Comparison

"A brand is a mark that identifies a property, and it is also a promise of quality, of style, and of a way of doing business."
—JAMES J. MAMMARELLA, *licensing and branding consultant and contributing writer to* Brandweek

"A brand is the imprint or impression left on constituents that an organization collectively possesses through the natural expression of its core values."
—DWAYNE FLINCHUM, *principal of Iridium Group Inc., a New York–based branding and design company*

"A promise—two words, eight letters—is *all* it takes. Don't make it complicated, black box, or mysterious."
—DAN ROSELLI, *president of Jambrose Marketing and former brand and advertising executive with Bank of America, General Mills, Colgate-Palmolive, and M&M/Mars*

"Any name, symbol, or identifying characteristic of a product or service that adds value that the product or service wouldn't otherwise have if it were generic."
—ABRAM SAUER, *brand analyst for Brandchannel.com*

Whatever your preferred definition, we all have or are a brand. This happens naturally the day we enter the world. The choice is either to take the "go with the flow" brand plan or to be conscious and strategic in your plan so your brand works toward your success. A triumphant brand is the by-product of a clear purpose, memorable personality, compelling distinction, and deliverable promise. Planning and management of these attributes directly affects the outcome of your Brain Tattoo.

Although the branding premise is supported by many industry sectors, some argue that the brand value is more applicable to consumer offerings than the business-to-business model. In my opinion, that's hogwash. Until we start selling and communicating with aliens, all businesses deal with and market to humans. They all have brains, some more used than others. They all have values and needs. The only real differences are their buying motives. If you are conscious of those motives and adjust your strategy accordingly, you can be successful. As I walk you through the process of brand building, I will point out important differences and nuances in the consumer and business markets.

Is There Ink on Your Tattoo?

Ask yourself these questions about your brand:

➤ Why are you/your company/your product here? (State your clear purpose.)
➤ How would someone describe you/your company/your product if he were fixing you up on a hot date? (Define your memorable personality.)
➤ How are you/your company/your product different from the others? (Explain your compelling distinction.)
➤ What will you/your company/your product promise me and deliver? (State a deliverable promise.)

After any tattoo is outlined, it must then be filled in with rich, potent colors that last—what is called *brand execution*. Without it, that great design and strategy just fade away.

Beyond the plan or outline, brands need product performance, innovation, and crisp names; eye-catching packaging; support by a committed team; and a communication program of reach, relevance, and frequency. The true essence of creating a great brand or Brain Tattoo is consciously molding, managing, and maximizing your desired mental imprint of your offering over an adequate period.

The Brands Tattooed on Your Brain

Coke. Nike. Starbucks. Did you ever wonder how those popular brand names happened? What if you could land a mental mark on your market's mind that would encourage buyers to pay more for your product, tell all their friends about how fabulous you are, and stick with you for a lifetime?

Okay, you may be thinking, "Those are mega-giant companies with ultra-humongous budgets—of course they can brand. But what about a new, young, and growing business with a micro-budget and limited staff?"

The Good News: Anyone Can Brand

Yes, many of those Fortune 500 companies have hefty budgets, but they also have markets the size of a small universe. Many great businesses and super-brands started locally, regionally, or in a small niche. In many cases, smaller businesses can actually do a better job of branding with less resources because they can control situations better, move more quickly, and also clearly define, geographically contain, or lifestyle-segment their market. Today anyone can brand and land successful Brain Tattoos. Branding is not just for big boys and big girls. And it's not rocket science, unless of course you are NASA.

Not only is branding not limited to big budgets and big companies, many of your competitors' branding is really bad. They don't get it. They still think it's about the cows, and some may soon be with them in the pasture. Branding is a *huge* opportunity and competitive advantage in all commercial sectors that sell products, services, or ideas to humans. Unless I missed something, that would include *your* business.

How many of your competitors use the same lame, meaningless words in their marketing collateral—phrases like *best quality, greatest performance,* or *dedicated service*—to build and communicate their foggy brand story? How many treat their business card as some cheap afterthought, a discount yellow pages ad, or worse, put an entire brochure on a 2-by-3.5-inch card? How many have never even heard their own phone answered after hours by some less-than-happy, mumbling, grumpy after-hours voice?

All these initiatives are part of the brand. These efforts can work brilliantly with you or simply drag your brand through the mud. It's your choice.

Where to Begin Your Branding Initiative

Many companies whine about not having a budget for branding when actually many have enough resources; they've just wasted tons of their cash, energy, and time on self-inflicted brand dilution. They act and spend before they think about the impact on their brands. Once branding plans are in place, all major business decisions need to consider the effect on the brand.

Do these excuses sound familiar? "We've got lots of great ideas. We want to please everyone, so our marketing efforts are all over the map." No time for a written plan. Afraid to rock the boat. "We follow the pack where it's comfortable." "We don't have time to engage the troops within our organization to be brand champions." And you're feeling a little brand blue? Hello! You should be feeling sick. That is the fast-track death wish of a brand destined to be on the History Channel. This is not where you want to be.

Granted, business leaders have extremely full plates. There's business development, finance, human resources, office therapist, and even marketing responsibilities. This branding stuff seems like a lot of work, and, besides, there's a good chance you're totally left-brained and the most creative thing you've ever done in your life is wear a red tie or bubble-gum lipstick. Not to worry. There is hope for you, and there are some very worthy reasons to get on the brand bandwagon now!

Growing a profitable business today means more than achieving market share. It means mastering mind share with strong Brain Tattoos, the pulsating imprint you plant on the minds of buyers, prospects, and stakeholders. Branding is so incredibly powerful yet a very simple process. A seat in the Branding Hall of Fame awaits you.

FROM THE BRAIN TRUST

Lead, Don't Follow

"Differentiate or die."
—JACK TROUT, *one of the godfathers of branding and author of* Differentiate or Die, Jack Trout on Strategy, *and* The New Positioning: The Latest on the World's #1 Business Strategy

"Be distinct or be extinct."
—TOM PETERS, *business management and change guru, author of* In Search of Excellence

Be Creative, but Keep Your Message Simple

Kick down the walls of boring and sameness and discover what's really so cool about your business and brand. Yes, this can be scary, but no real legends in business ever lacked courage.

At the same time, keep in mind that we live in a time of information chaos. Consumers are assaulted by truckloads of branding mumbo-jumbo every day. Make it easier on your customers and yourself by executing a simple, single-focused approach, and your story will permeate deeply in the minds of your market and will not wash off with time.

Branding: Not Just for Products

Most companies have many incredible branding opportunities right under their noses, but if those opportunities are not products on a shelf, the company executives don't see them. Remember, Brain Tattoos are the emotional connections between a buyer and the seller and are generally sealed with an extra layer of added perceived value.

Branding is not limited to products. If your business sells franchises, you can brand your training programs—how about something like The System Squad, for example? If you have a secret item that is "the punch" to your product, why not brand the ingredient, like JamminJuice? And then maybe you can license it to other products. How about you? Professionals, business leaders, and individuals can be branded, too. What about an annual event you produce? Coin a killer name, like Houston's HomeSpot. Build up the brand equity and you have a brand-new asset. (For more information about what you can brand, see Chapter 1.)

Branding: A Family Affair

As I mentioned earlier, most companies, professionals, services, and products have some sort of natural brand—the one they are born with; the sum of all of their activities, behaviors, and attributes. Some of these brands are fortunate enough to evolve from this unconscious state to a very strategic, purposeful Brain Tattoo, while others never tap their full potential. I like to organize and think of brands as a family affair.

Parent Brands

If you are a holding entity of one or more business units, you are a parent brand (or as I call it, the "mother" brand). Examples are

Procter & Gamble and Johnson & Johnson. Many corporations fall in this segment. Like your brand offspring, parent brands need to have a clear purpose, market position, personality, and promise to compete successfully. These are not necessarily the same as your kids.

Kid Brands

Next, come the kids. These independent brands have their own set of attributes. Sometimes there are obvious, inherent family values passed down from the parent brand. Sometimes it's hard to recognize who their parents are. For example, Altoids, the highly hip, irreverent brand, is owned by Kraft Foods.

Cousin Brands

Brand cousins are extensions of a brand, like American Express Green, American Express Blue, and American Express Gold. They generally have a common name component or theme, but address a niche market's needs.

Licensed Brands

Once a brand has earned significant brand equity in the market, it can start building partnerships with complementary brands. Agreements are generally structured for brand consumption, royalties/compensation, and brand usage and identity control rights. A classic example is when McDonald's licensed its fun, family fast-food brand to Wal-Mart, allowing the retailer the opportunity to sell McKids clothing. It was a natural fit for both parties. Successful partnerships can generate significant on-going royalties, extend the reach of the brand to new market segments, and add to the brand's visibility.

The Role of Licensing. Brand licensing has reached epic proportions across many segments of business, from software architecture to fashion, food, and commercial and consumer services. Under a typical win-win scenario of licensing, each brand partner, in the short term, gives up a portion of the revenues it could potentially gain on its own. In return, each brand partner acquires any of several valuable things, such as the extension of the brand into new categories, acquisition of new consumer and client segments, entry into new markets, gain in competitive market share, higher profit margins, or infrastructure cost-savings in manufacturing, research, marketing, and distribution. According to James J.

Mammarella, a licensing and branding strategist and contributor to *Brandweek,* "Ultimately, brand licensing can keep a licensee more competitive and up-to-date. Brand licensing can provide a licenser the benefits of a secure revenue stream in the form of royalty payments and the associated guarantees."

Branding: It's About Emotions

Extraordinary branding and super-strong Brain Tattoos connect with the buyer's core values and deepest desires. Brands are about a relationship, not a transaction. Branding is an opportunity for you to tell a story about your offering to the market.

Dark, rich tattoo ink comes only to those brand leaders who will step away from the market pack and distance themselves from the obvious logic of their offering, the attributes that rationally describe their product or service. Since the odds are that your competitors will stick with the bland, overused approach and blend into the deep forest of look-alikes, your brand will stand out from the rest.

I'm not suggesting you omit those left-brain attributes and features. I am recommending you go deeper into your creative well and first build a brand foundation that is emotional, heartfelt, and compelling, then weave the other features nicely into your ongoing dialogue with your buyer.

According to Marc Gobé, author of *Emotional Branding* (one of my favorite books on the subject), "An emotional branding approach quite simply is the crucial defining element that separates success from indifference in the marketplace."[1] His book comprehensively explores how demographics are changing and new cultures are emerging, and it features real winners in this thriving emotional economy.

Connect Through Emotions, Confirm Through Reason

In other words, sometimes the best direction for your brand may be miles away from the most likely or obvious side of your offering. Get emotional, find the psychological needs and desires of your buyers that best match your core self, and fill those needs. Align your promise with the buyer's deepest feelings. Land the Brain Tattoo where it matters.

Think about a few extremely successful consumer brands such as Rolex, Nike, and Apple Computer. If they built their brand purely on features, they would look just like the others. Instead, they focus on an emotional need and desire and establish a bond with buyers who share those values. For instance:

Brand	Emotional Need/Desire
Rolex watches	Status, prestige
Nike shoes/clothing	Achievement, joy of the experience
Apple computers	Being different, creative, and hip

Think, Feel Before Function

Connecting with buyers' needs is not an easy process. In fact, for many it's a radical shift in thinking, especially for those left-brainers with regimented, operational, conformist mind-sets. This change in behavior can be learned. It just takes a bit of discipline, a dash of open-mindedness, and a ton of courage.

As humans, we all have instinctive and culture-hardened value systems. Most of us have a mix of different values. Some of our values evolve with life experiences. Some remain as permanent as dry cement during our whole life.

Let's explore just a few common values that are inherent in the human race:

Achievement	Dominance	Power
Adventure/Risk	Duty	Protection
Artistic	Expression/Creativity	Recognition
Authority	Fame	Security
Balance	Family	Self-expression
Community/Belonging	Fun	Spirituality
Competition	Hipness	Stability
Contribution	Independence	Status
Control	Learning	Tradition

Now think about a brand that you personally like and buy. What value does it deliver for you? That's the "value fix" and probably a strong driving factor in your buying process. Next, try to break down the primary connection (value) into many smaller, supporting triggers, like adjectives, stories, and communication schemes. The theme should become apparent; but, perhaps most important, the thinking should reflect a strategy ideas that can be applied to any brand makeup. Some classic examples of emotional branding include:

➤ **Harley-Davidson.** The Harley brand is not about a means of transportation or sturdy shock absorbers. It's about an attitude of full-blown freedom. It's about unleashing the rebel inside, living your wild side, even if you are an Ivy League, conservative-on-the-surface, over-sixty-year-old female lawyer.

➤ **Victoria's Secret.** Undergarments have been around for centuries, a pure fashion commodity if ever I've seen one. Add some value/desire and personality (adventure, recognition, self-expression, and lots of fun) to drive your advertising and—wow!—you have an international brand sensation. Men and women are drawn to these emotional magnets. You'd better believe there are major Brain Tattoos at work here.

Whatever industry you operate in, chances are the marketplace is noisy, crowded, cluttered, confusing, and full of way too many products and services that look and act alike. This condition has been referred to as the "sea of sameness." I like to call it the ocean of lameness. Although many businesses stay in this arena of no compelling brand or, at best, weak brand status, the real winners stand out with a purpose, are memorable, and deliver on emotional needs and desires. They are masters of the Brain Tattoo and enjoy prominent and profitable stature in their chosen playing field.

Is It "Brand-Able?" Ten Questions to Ask Before You Begin

When most people think of commercial branding, they recall a product on a grocery store shelf or a big company brand. While both of these examples are accurate, there are many other branding opportunities within organizations. Remember, a brand is the sum of an entity, a mental connection that creates a loyal bond with a buyer/prospect and the offering, and it often includes an added layer of perceived value. This same concept applies to other business matters: adding value, instilling confidence, building trust, creating loyalty, reducing risk, and stimulating a buying preference.

Often consumers will pay more for branded goods, believing there is more value delivered and less risk in their buying decision. For these reasons, branding *beyond* the product can make good business sense.

As I speak to businesspeople around the country and work with them to answer the question "What is brandable in their business model?" I recommend that they answer a series of questions about why they want to brand something. For example, by branding X:

1. Will you add value to the organization?
2. Will customers pay more for a purchase?
3. Will you add stature to your offering?
4. Will it differentiate your offering from competitors?
5. Will it aid in the selling process?
6. Will it build customer loyalty?
7. Will you attract positive media interest?
8. Will you create licensing opportunities?
9. Will you attract meaningful strategic alliances?
10. Will you attract and keep top talent?

What Can Be Branded?

In most situations, a brand is a thing rather than an activity or experience. Here are some examples of things that can be branded. They are real examples from a mix of large and small companies, so they demonstrate that the strategy can be applied to any size company.

Company Brand

A company brand is often the "mother" of all the organization's brands. Sometimes it acts as a holding unit for many business interests, and sometimes it is the driving business interest. For instance, Method Products (www.methodhome.com), a young San Francisco company, has transformed mundane cleaning products into a collection of beautifully designed, leave-on-the-counter accessories. All of their products fall under the company brand name. Whether you use a company brand or individual brands, a brand should have a purpose, personality, promise, and point of difference among its competitors.

Ingredient Brand

An ingredient brand is precisely what its name implies: an ingredient or element of a product that has its own brand. Ingredient branding can serve as an added strategy to build a primary brand or as a way to differentiate a commodity. A good example is Arm & Hammer Baking

Soda (www.armandhammer.com), which first emerged as a product with a pure kitchen purpose. Today, it adds value to many products like toothpaste and detergent. Another case in point is Teflon (www.teflon .com), which is listed in *Guinness Book of World Records* as the slipperiest material in the world and is found in more than twenty-five product categories.

Ingredient branding certainly is not restricted to the consumer market. Business, industrial, and technology interests are jumping on the brand wagon, from the Intel computer microchip to NIKEAIR technology found in Cole Haan shoes. So what exactly is NIKEAIR technology? I turned to a shoe expert site (http://shoeme.com) and learned that NIKEAIR is pressurized gas inside a tough yet flexible urethane bag. It reduces the force of impact and then immediately recovers to its original shape and volume, ready for the next blow.

Considering an Ingredient Brand? Landor, an international branding consultancy group based in San Francisco, recommends that you ask yourself the following questions:

➤ Is the ingredient a point of entry in your product category?
➤ Is there consumer demand for the ingredient?
➤ Does the ingredient fit in with the overall strategy of the host brand, or will the new ingredient detract from the host brand's message?
➤ Can the host brand live up to the added promise of the ingredient?
➤ How versatile is the ingredient? Is it used in other product categories?
➤ What other product brands are using the ingredient? What are their brand images?
➤ How risky is the ingredient? Are there potential problems/ risks that could taint the credibility of your product?
➤ Is the ingredient new or established in the marketplace?
➤ Do you anticipate any supply-related problems that could affect the production and overall sales of your product (e.g., occasional supply shortages of an ingredient that is used in a variety of products)?
➤ How expensive is the ingredient to license? Do you have sufficient resources to properly support the implementation and continued consumer promotion of the ingredient brand?

➤ Will you lose consumers because of the resulting price increase?

Answering these questions will help you decide whether ingredient branding is the right strategy for you, or if you should think twice before jumping on the ingredient branding brandwagon.[2]

Organization Brand

An organization brand in many cases generally refers to a not-for-profit group, special interest consortium, cause, or trade association. Generally, the same principles apply to creating this brand; modifications may be necessary in executing the brand strategy based on the organization's goals and sensitivity to commercial practices.

Dwayne Flinchum, principal at Iridium Group Inc., noted that his firm has seen a broadening of the acceptance of branding disciplines with his nonprofit clients. "They realize the value of their own brands and are paying more attention to their image-building efforts and programs." The Nature Conservancy (www.tnc.org), one of Iridium's clients, is a stellar example of a rebranding effort that beautifully adhered to the organization's core values and created a consistent visual identity that resonates through all points of contact. The initiative included an annual report and other publications, Web site, merchandise, and even a brand book to guide usage and understanding of the brand for staff and promotional partners.

Service Brand

FedEx (www.fedex.com) is a family of companies forming a global network of specialized services—transportation, information, international trade support, and supply chain services. While the main brand, FedEx, is a major Brain Tattoo, the company sub-brands its services using different names and a distinct color scheme. Examples are FedEx Express, FedEx Ground, FedEx Freight, and FedEx Custom Critical.

Event Brand

In 1877, a few hundred spectators watched tennis in a garden party atmosphere; today, Wimbledon (www.wimbledon.org) is a highly professional tournament attracting more than 500,000 people to the Centre Court and, through the press, radio, Internet, and television, a following of millions throughout the world. How does that happen? The same way product branding does. Early on, the defined standards guide the brand. It's then built with a consistent story and backed by communication execution that grows every year. Does your organization have an event worthy of brand prominence?

Team Brand

Branding a team—whether it's a professional football team like my favorite Tampa Bay Buccaneers (www.tampabaybucs.com), an elite research and development troop within an organization, or two striking teens named Mary-Kate and Ashley (www.mary-kateandashley.com) who capture the hearts of teenagers around the world—offers many business and income possibilities. Branded teams can benefit from licensing or from charging a premium for services or products.

Many professional service businesses miss this branding opportunity, especially when they provide a service that many others do. By branding the intelligence, or even the personality of a team, the team brand factor can become a point of differentiation and a selling strategy to get the next big deal.

Destination Brand

Branding a place or destination gives people a reason to visit. Whether it's a center for the arts or a community development, branding a place solidifies the environment and defines its personality and being. One of my favorite examples is an area in Houston, Texas, called Uptown Houston (www.uptown-houston.com). Since 1975, this nonprofit organization has been committed to serving the business and residential interests of this destination. Branding efforts have promoted the area, encouraged economic growth and redevelopment, and facilitated funding to create an urban center of exceptional beauty, unparalleled amenities, and a dynamic business center. From its Web site to events, street signage to publications, Uptown Houston is a divine destination brand.

Service or Maintenance Agreement Brand

Getting buyers to commit to pay for product insurance or advanced maintenance can be a difficult sell. By branding the protection, one can build trust and add another layer of value to the proposition.

AppleCare Protection Plan (www.apple.com) promises long-term peace of mind. For a fee, the service extends the complimentary coverage to three years of world-class support. The plan includes expert telephone assistance, on-site repairs for desktop computers, global repair coverage for portable computers, Web-based resources, and TechTool Deluxe from Micromat—all for one price. The concept of branding an agreement can add needed credibility and ease of purchasing to a service—and it can also be a good, added cash flow channel.

Program Brand

Within a company brand, an organization can brand a program, adding value and identity to the offering. A branded program can reward loyalty, volume buying, and even prepaid purchasing.

Southwest Airlines (www.southwest.com) has not only branded the company well, but also introduced its Southwest Rapid Rewards program with significant success, achieving landed brand status. Staying true to its parent brand reputation for simplicity, Southwest awards travelers with free travel. Eliminating familiar complexities and restrictions common with other loyalty programs, Southwest Airlines states, "Life can be complicated; flying for free shouldn't be." They also carry the message one step further with a branded newsletter called "Rapid Report."

Certification Brand

Evaluating credentials, credibility, and trust are all important elements in the buyers' decision-making process. Branding a certification can raise the value of your promise, giving your qualifications added merit and an official status. This type of branding works well in both consumer and business environments. Once a certification program is designed, a brand can then be communicated with a logo, seal, crest, or diploma to substantiate the value further.

Mitch Meyerson, founder and CEO of Guerrilla Marketing International (www.gmarketingcoach.com), offers his market (business coaches) an added level of worth and credibility with his Guerrilla Marketing Coach Certification Program. The certification demonstrates completion of an intensive twelve-week program and membership in an elite group of other practitioners from more than eighty countries around the world.

Bundle of Services Brand

Many companies are branding collections of products or bundles of services. By brand-naming a group of products, the organization has an opportunity to tell a story about an offering and provide buyers with an identity they can emotionally connect to and establish affinity with.

For over a hundred years, Thomasville Furniture (www.thomasville .com) has been an enduring home furnishings brand in its own right. In 1999 it introduced, to much acclaim, a licensed collection named after renowned American author Ernest Hemingway. Following the success of that collection, in 2003 Thomasville launched the elegant Bogart collection, inspired by the life and times of screen legend and cultural icon Humphrey Bogart. The furniture, like Bogie himself, is inherently classic and romantic. In each case, the men's style and the nostalgia for an era helped define the product's persona and enhanced the brand.

Verizon has branded a bundle of services under the Verizon Freedom Plan (www.verizon.com). By packaging and branding these services, Verizon gives customers pricing incentives (a flat fee) and convenience while connecting through the emotional value of freedom. The ad copy reads, UNLIMIT YOURSELF.

Publication Brand

A publication—whether an industry-focused report or a magazine geared to a segment of consumers—is a choice avenue for branding. Just by the nature of multiple issues or occurrences, publications give brand leaders a consistent path and connection to their audience.

Mental_floss (www.mentalfloss.com), a new brand in intellectual reading, promises to make people feel smart again. The publication's mission is to take the chore out of learning by combining education and entertainment in an online magazine. Eventually, you may see mental_floss as a host brand to many channels of intelligence.

Seth Godin (www.sethgodin.com), author of four worldwide bestsellers and renowned agent of change, recently launched not only a great book, but also a great book brand, Purple Cow. I first saw the book on the cover of *Fast Company* magazine. After reading the article, readers were invited to order their *free* book before it was available to the rest of the world. The book was shipped in a milk carton with a purple cow patch. That's what I call smart milkin' of a brand for lots of future moola.

Personal Brand

If you compete with anyone for anything, you need to establish a trust factor in your selling process, and credibility is an important attribute to your marketing. Just like the products on the grocery store shelves that are vying for attention in that cluttered, aggressive environment, you need to apply the same branding concept to marketing yourself, or what I refer to as a Brand *Moi*.

People with strong personal brands are more likely to enjoy their life journey, earn more, achieve ambitious goals, and attract superstar members to their team or cause. Two personal brands I admire are Katie Couric, NBC's *Today* show host, and Donald Trump, business mogul and star of *The Apprentice*.

Katie's bubbly girl-next-door persona exudes her brand. For two decades we've all watched her grow; we relate to her challenges and laud her incredible success. Her visual style is consistently full of energy, and her professional achievements earn our trust. Her story resonates with millions of people who share her same values.

Donald Trump, bad hair and all, has been tattooed in many of our minds. Respect his wealth or despise his ego and high-profile holdings, Trump is the image of American business success. Thanks to the hit reality show *The Apprentice,* use of the phrase "You're fired" adds more "Donald" power to a well-established brand.

Membership or Club Brand

Since branding adds an extra layer of value to an offering, branding a membership or club is a natural. Marcelina (www.marcelinaclub.com) is truly a branded oasis of serenity. The exclusive club for women is located inside one of Tampa's oldest and grandest mansions. Built in 1897, the fully restored mansion offers meeting rooms, elegant dining, a full-service spa, gift boutique, and speaker series. From the flag that adorns the building to the branded products and apparel, Marcelina is the perfect place to enrich one's life, as well as the lives of others. With a brand purpose of creating balance and fulfillment and encouraging philanthropic activities, Marcelina will soon be extending the brand to young women through its Marcelinagirl.com programs.

FROM THE BRAIN TRUST

How Has Branding Changed?

"The speed at which information is now disseminated is fantastic. What's more, this speed increases a hundred-fold every year as more and more people become wired. Just a half decade ago, a brand could feel fairly confident about how much of its own image it fully controlled. However, today, information about a brand—positive or not—can make its way around the world four times before the brand manager even has a hint about what's going on. The half-life of any one group's control on information will continue to decrease in the future, which, more than likely, will necessitate media and Web monitoring departments in organizations to watch, in real time, how a brand's image is faring."

—ABRAM SAUER, *brand analyst for Brandchannel.com*

"Companies now take branding seriously rather than viewing it as a necessary evil of their marketing efforts . . . [I]t is increasingly conventional wisdom that brands are of exceptional importance. Additionally, as companies move from owning their own factories to sourcing, they have shifted their emphasis to branding. It used to be that companies were in the business of turning raw materials into commodities. They later turned commodities into consumer products. Now, post–WWII and since the opening of China, companies that sell consumer products are simply in the business of designing and marketing what foreign factories produce."

—SETH M. SIEGEL, *cofounder of The Beanstalk Group, a national licensing agency, and contributing writer to* Brandweek

"More and more very small companies understand that they are, in fact, a brand, and that they'd best tend to making it a good one."

—JOE CALLOWAY, *author of* Becoming a Category of One: How Extraordinary Companies Transcend Commodity and Defy Comparison

"Business leaders are becoming more and more reliant on mass media vehicles to build brand, which is not good. Brands are built with a relevant and differentiated promise brought to life through associates, environment, and experiences. Mass media can only communicate the promise; the company must be prepared to deliver the promise."

—DAN ROSELLI, *brand consultant and former brand executive with Bank of America*

Patterns of Success

Brands are like children. They start small, they are all unique, sometimes they can make you crazy, but with good parenting and support, they can grow up to be something really special. You'll be proud to say, "Yep, they're mine and I love 'em."

Brain Tattooing is exciting, exhilarating, and fun, and it can bring you much joy. It is my goal to open your mind, challenge your thinking, and kick you in the butt and amp up your attitude about branding. Vast opportunities await you.

Five-Second Brand Bites—An Indelible Impression

1. Brands are the sum of your [company's/product's] purpose, personality, position, and promise.
2. Brands *connect* through emotion and *confirm* through reason.
3. Brands are about relationships, not transactions.
4. Brand leaders don't follow the pack.
5. Brand leaders breathe their brand every day.

End Notes

1. Marc Gobé, *Emotional Branding: The New Paradigm for Connecting Brands to People* (New York: Allworth Press, 2001), p. ix. Used by permission of the author.
2. The questions are from Landor Associates, "Ingredient Branding: Does What's Inside Really Matter?" December 1998 (available at http://www.landor.com/index.cfm?fuseaction = cBranding.getArticle &storyid = 134). Copyright © Landor.com. Used by permission.

chapter 2

Brand Checkup: Is Your Tattoo One Big Smudge?

Is your tattoo ink rich with color—your brand difference, personality, and promise? Does the design symbolize who you are, or is it one big smudge of message misfortune?

The strength and potency of a brand can be affected by so many uncontrollable factors: the environment, the economy, and social influences, in addition to the controllable decisions made by management and marketing teams. Market conditions change, new media are introduced, stuff happens, and aggressive competition is always out there.

Taking your brand's pulse with a regular checkup is vital to sustained growth. When I work with companies on new brands, rebranding, or brand augmentation, I conduct a simple brand assessment. I call this nonscientific tool The Tattoo Test. Regular use of this test can help uncover a new brand or brand extension's potential, unleash opportunities for a current brand, provide additional analysis for determining a brand's financial value, or serve as a wake-up call that your brand is in big trouble. If you see an area that needs work, act on it!

The More Brand Assets, the More Valuable the Brand

Just like big firms, privately held and small businesses should consider brands as financial assets when selling, merging, or acquiring business units. To the best of my knowledge, there is no one formula to value a brand. Because of the range of objectives and factors in financial brand valuation, you should consult your accounting professional for the best method for your situation. However, some things can add more dollar value to a brand's worth—for example, the number of public impressions via positive publicity and sponsorships, the amount of money spent on advertising, and the number of nonpaid endorsements.

How Strong Is Your Brand?

"Google yourself and see what you find. While very unscientific, this sort of early approach will give you an immediate—and inexpensive—idea of what issues are attached to your name. Next, I would recommend looking at who your target is. Is your brand aimed primarily at young men? If so, then you should go hang out with young men and see what they think. Lastly, if your brand is big enough, recruiting professionals to do a full analysis of your brand's *potency* is probably a useful step."
    —ABRAM SAUER, *brand analyst for Brandchannel.com, international branding information exchange*

Seth Siegel, licensing expert, cofounder of The Beanstalk Group, and contributing writer to *Brandweek,* says it is nearly impossible to define a brand assessment. *BusinessWeek* has developed criteria in conjunction with Interbrand, an international branding consultancy. Others have also come up with brand valuation approaches. While I respect these efforts, I remain skeptical that these systems really capture brand value. Great brands, like your best friends, have that *je ne sais quoi* quality, which is elusive and nearly impossible to define. If you can tell me what it is you love about your best friend, I suspect you could then do the same for a brand. For now, brands remain on the balance sheet under the category of "intangible."

Is the Ink Fading?

To assess possible factors in brand dilution or value reduction, ask yourself these questions:

➤ Have you recalled any products?
➤ Have you poorly managed a crisis in the media?

- ➤ Have you been involved in negative publicity about your brand, its leadership, or its holding company?
- ➤ Have operational issues had a negative impact on your brand?
- ➤ Have significant external market challenges negatively impacted your brand?
- ➤ Have labor issues had a negative impact on your brand?
- ➤ Have management changes had a negative impact on your brand? (For example, did your CEO just get indicted?)

Negative events can dilute a brand's stature. Handle these events with timely and brand-sensitive responses. Because a brand is a precious asset, it is essential to keep a careful eye on how the brand is fairing. If, for any reason, the ink on your tattoo begins to fade, take immediate steps to remedy the situation.

Tattoo Tests

Whether your organization is a start-up or thriving business with many brands, all business leaders should periodically perform a Tattoo Test or some similar assessment to determine the potency of their brand and the depth of the channel (i.e., retail, wholesale, licensing, online) and its reach, visibility level, and impact on their business model.

While this test addresses many elements of a solid brand, it is not a quantitative study. Within every industry and market scope, there are specific issues and factors that may need to be added to enhance the validity of this exercise.

I have created two versions of the Tattoo Test, one for consumer brands and one for business-to-business (B2B) brands. For a brand that is involved in both markets, simply take both tests.

Test all your brands individually, including your organizational or company brand, product brands, service brands, event brands, ingredient brands, and so on. Leadership or personal branding will be addressed in Chapter 3.

TATTOO TEST: CONSUMER BRANDS

Answer yes or no to each of the questions, then see how your brand scores in the significance summary at the end.

Brand Planning	YES	NO
Have you documented your short- and long-term business goals with accountable measures?	❑	❑
If so, have you updated your short- and long-term business goals in the past twelve months?	❑	❑
Do you have an action plan with strategies and tactics to achieve these goals?	❑	❑
Does your brand have an annual research plan/budget?	❑	❑

Does your research include the following:

	YES	NO
Written polls?	❑	❑
Focus studies?	❑	❑
Web surveys?	❑	❑
Live surveys?	❑	❑
Mall surveys?	❑	❑
Calling up a customer and having a chat?	❑	❑
Playing the role of a customer and walking through your buying process?	❑	❑

	YES	NO
Do you assess your top-three competing brands at least annually?	❑	❑
Do you send out a mystery shopper to experience your top-three competing brands at least annually?	❑	❑

Brand Category	YES	NO
Are you the market share leader in your category?	❑	❑
Have you created a new category?	❑	❑

Brand Difference	YES	NO
Does your brand own a unique distinction in the market?	❑	❑
Can you describe what differentiates your brand from your competitors' in fewer than ten words?	❑	❑

Brand Communication	YES	NO
Does your brand name stand out among your competitors?	❑	❑
Is at least one of your Web addresses consistent with your brand name?	❑	❑

Brand Communication	YES	NO
Is the brand's graphic identity distinguishable from the competition?	❏	❏
Is the brand's graphic identity effective in all media (e.g., print, fax, Web, packaging, etc.)?	❏	❏
Does your organization adhere to a graphics standards program for the brand's identity?	❏	❏

Phrases That Pay	YES	NO
Does your brand have a tagline and/or positioning statement that is current and relevant?	❏	❏
Are taglines used in a consistent manner?	❏	❏

Brand Promise	YES	NO
Does your brand communicate a clear promise and deliver on it?	❏	❏

Brand Experience	YES	NO
Does your brand deliver a memorable experience:		
Before the market buys?	❏	❏
During the transaction?	❏	❏
After the transaction?	❏	❏
Does your organization breathe the brand through all points of buyer contact?	❏	❏
Does your organization breathe the brand through all channels of distribution?	❏	❏
Do you have an active loyalty program for your best customers?	❏	❏

Brand Culture	YES	NO
Is your brand embraced and executed in all departments?	❏	❏
Does your organization host brand events for its employees?	❏	❏
Is your brand built into all employee training and recruitment programs, including manuals?	❏	❏

Brand Culture

	YES	NO
Is the brand message apparent in your organization's physical environment (e.g., lobby, workroom, signage, etc.)?	❏	❏
Do you have an active reward program for employees who are brand ambassadors?	❏	❏

Brand Reach

	YES	NO
Are your market segments clearly defined and prioritized by geographic, psychographic, and demographic profiles?	❏	❏

Brand Story

Is your brand story/message apparent and consistent in your:

	YES	NO
Print advertising?	❏	❏
Broadcast advertising?	❏	❏
Radio ads?	❏	❏
Web site?	❏	❏
Web marketing?	❏	❏
Print collateral?	❏	❏
Packaging?	❏	❏
Merchandising?	❏	❏
Point of purchase?	❏	❏
Phone system?	❏	❏
Uniforms?	❏	❏
Delivery vehicles?	❏	❏
Outdoor/signage?	❏	❏
External publications?	❏	❏
Internal publications?	❏	❏
Public shows?	❏	❏
Events?	❏	❏
Promotional items?	❏	❏
Employee relations?	❏	❏
Shareholder relations?	❏	❏
Government relations?	❏	❏
Community/industry relations (i.e., sponsorships)?	❏	❏
Media relations?	❏	❏

Brand Awareness

	YES	NO
Do you invest at least 5 percent to 10 percent of your operating budget in brand building?	❏	❏

Do you invest in targeted advertising in:

	YES	NO
Print?	❏	❏
Broadcast?	❏	❏

	Yes	NO
Radio?	☐	☐
Web marketing?	☐	☐
Print collateral?	☐	☐
Outdoor/signage?	☐	☐
External publications?	☐	☐
Internal publications?	☐	☐
Public shows?	☐	☐
Events?	☐	☐
Word-of-mouth marketing?	☐	☐
Promotional items?	☐	☐
Shareholder relations?	☐	☐
Government relations?	☐	☐
Community/industry relations (i.e., sponsorships)?	☐	☐
Media relations?	☐	☐

SIGNIFICANCE

Count the number of "yes" responses and score your test as follows:

60–77 *(A Landed Brand or Solid Brain Tattoo)*
Congratulations! You are breathing your brand. It's established, strong, and working for you. Keep your eye on those outside factors, modify as needed, and pat yourself and your staff on the back. Great job!

30–59 *(A Baby Brand Ready to Be Born)*
You have the seeds to grow a strong brand. However, you've got work to do. Start today. Invest time in brand planning, continue nurturing, amp up your commitment, and add some additional branding fuel to your engine.

0–29 *(Barely a Brand)*
You are missing huge opportunities to expand your success. All facets of your business may become more difficult. Customer acquisition may rise along with customer defection. What are you waiting for?

TATTOO TEST: BUSINESS-TO-BUSINESS BRANDS

Answer yes or no to each of the questions, then see how your brand scores in the significance summary at the end.

Brand Planning	YES	NO
Have you documented your short- and long-term business goals with accountable measures?	❏	❏
If so, have you updated your short- and long-term business goals in the past twelve months?	❏	❏
Do you have an action plan with strategies and tactics to achieve these goals?	❏	❏
Does your brand have an annual research plan/budget?	❏	❏

Does your research include the following:

	YES	NO
Written polls?	❏	❏
Focus studies?	❏	❏
Web surveys?	❏	❏
Live surveys?	❏	❏
Trade shows surveys?	❏	❏
Calling customers for a chat?	❏	❏
Playing customer and walking through your buying process?	❏	❏

	YES	NO
Do you assess your top-three competing brands at least annually?	❏	❏
Do you send out a mystery shopper to experience your top-three competing brands at least annually?	❏	❏

Brand Category	YES	NO
Are you the market share leader in your category?	❏	❏
Have you created a new category?	❏	❏

Brand Difference	YES	NO
Does your brand own a unique distinction in the market?	❏	❏
Can you describe what differentiates your brand from your competitors' in fewer than ten words?	❏	❏

Brand Communication	YES	NO
Does your brand name stand out among your competition?	❏	❏
Is at least one of your Web addresses consistent with your brand name?	❏	❏

Brand Communication	YES	NO
Is the brand's graphic identity distinguishable from the competition?	❑	❑
Is the brand's graphic identity effective in all media (e.g., print, fax, Web, packaging, etc.)?	❑	❑
Does your organization adhere to a graphics standards program for the brand's identity?	❑	❑

Phrases That Pay	YES	NO
Does your brand have a tagline and/or positioning statement that is current and relevant?	❑	❑
Are taglines used in a consistent manner?	❑	❑

Brand Promise	YES	NO
Does your brand communicate a clear promise and deliver on it?	❑	❑

Brand Experience	YES	NO
Does your brand deliver a memorable experience:		
Before the market buys?	❑	❑
During the transaction?	❑	❑
After the transaction?	❑	❑
Does your organization breathe the brand through all points of buyer contact?	❑	❑
Does your organization breathe the brand through all channels of distribution?	❑	❑
Do you have an active loyalty program for your best customers?	❑	❑

Brand Culture	YES	NO
Is your brand embraced and executed in all departments?	❑	❑
Does your organization host brand events for its employees?	❑	❑
Is your brand built into all employee training and recruitment programs, including manuals?	❑	❑

Brand Culture	YES	NO
Is the brand message apparent in your organization's physical environment (e.g., lobby, workroom, signage, etc.)?	❏	❏
Do you have an active reward program for employees who are brand ambassadors?	❏	❏

Brand Reach	YES	NO
Are your market segments clearly defined and prioritized by geographic, psychographic, and demographic profiles?	❏	❏

Brand Story	YES	NO
Is your brand story/message apparent and consistent in your:		
Print advertising?	❏	❏
Broadcast advertising?	❏	❏
Radio ads?	❏	❏
Web site?	❏	❏
Web marketing?	❏	❏
Print collateral?	❏	❏
Packaging?	❏	❏
Merchandising?	❏	❏
Point of purchase?	❏	❏
Phone system?	❏	❏
Uniforms?	❏	❏
Delivery vehicles?	❏	❏
Outdoor/signage?	❏	❏
External publications?	❏	❏
Internal publications?	❏	❏
Trade shows?	❏	❏
Events?	❏	❏
Promotional items?	❏	❏
Employee relations?	❏	❏
Shareholder relations?	❏	❏
Government relations?	❏	❏
Community/industry relations (i.e., sponsorships)?	❏	❏
Media relations?	❏	❏

Brand Awareness	YES	NO
Do you invest at least 5 percent to 10 percent of your operating budget in brand building?	❏	❏
Do you invest in targeted advertising in:		
Print?	❏	❏
Broadcast?	❏	❏

	Yes	NO
Radio?	❑	❑
Web marketing?	❑	❑
Print collateral?	❑	❑
Outdoor/signage?	❑	❑
External publications?	❑	❑
Internal publications?	❑	❑
Trade shows?	❑	❑
Events?	❑	❑
Word-of-mouth marketing?	❑	❑
Promotional items?	❑	❑
Shareholder relations?	❑	❑
Government relations?	❑	❑
Community/industry relations (i.e., sponsorships)?	❑	❑
Media relations	❑	❑

SIGNIFICANCE

Count how many times you responded "yes" and score your test as follows:

60–77 *(A Landed Brand or Solid Brain Tattoo)*
Congratulations! You are breathing your brand. It's established, strong, and working for you. Keep your eye on those outside factors, modify as needed, and pat yourself and your staff on the back. Great job!

30–59 *(A Baby Brand Ready to Be Born)*
You have the seeds to grow a strong brand. However, you've got work to do. Start today. Invest time in brand planning, continue nurturing, amp up your commitment, and add some additional branding fuel to your engine.

0–29 *(Barely a Brand)*
You are missing huge opportunities to expand your success. All facets of your business may become more difficult. Customer acquisition may rise along with customer defection. What are you waiting for?

Brain Tattooing is a very much an in-the-moment business discipline, a conscious state of awareness and flexibility that allows you to react to uncontrollable market circumstances. The more you stay on top of your game with regular brand checkups, the more likely your brand will stay on your customers' minds in a positive, dominant manner.

Five-Second Brand Bites—Keep Your Tattoo Vibrant

1. Brands are *assets;* treat them as such.
2. The strength and potency of a brand can be affected by many uncontrollable factors.
3. Brands should be looked after daily and formally assessed annually.
4. If you learn something from this assessment, act on it. Either improve it, extend it, or dump it.
5. Negative events can dilute a brand; handle with timely and brand-sensitive responses.

chapter 3

Brand *Moi:* Your Personal Brand

Chapter 2 explored all the various opportunities for branding within an organization and ended with the idea of branding a person. Most of us recognize branded celebrities such as Venus and Serena Williams, Jewel, and Dr. Phil. No one doubts that they make a ton of money and have more opportunities than they know what to do with. Clearly, they all understand the process and value of branding—just ask them about their last endorsement contract.

Personal branding is vital for:

➤ Salespeople and sales professionals
➤ Business development directors, rainmakers, and all marketing types
➤ Consultants, coaches, and trainers
➤ Experts, authors, speakers, and gurus
➤ Company dragon slayers, change agents, managers, and executives
➤ Industry renegades, pioneers, and leaders
➤ Future and current politicians
➤ Entertainers, pro athletes, comedians, or wannabes
➤ Just about everyone else who wants something he or she doesn't have

Companies and organizations worldwide spend enormous resources on building their product's brand. They know that a sound brand adds value to their existence, stimulates loyalty, attracts great employees, and enhances profits.

We are all "a product" in a sense. We sell, we pitch, we persuade, and we advocate for stuff that is a part of a greater plan—which will, we hope, fulfill a dream or take us across a finish line.

Think back to your high school days. Remember the class clown, the book nerd, or the country club kid. In a sense, all those kids were branded. You knew who they were and exactly what they were about. A Brand *Moi* is your personal mark that symbolizes who you are and what you stand for and defines your unique contribution to the world. It does not matter whether you are a salesperson, a community leader, a business expert, an industry professional, or a college student, a personal brand can be your ticket to greater success.

Why You Need to Be a Brand

What does your brand say about you? Is it a strong brand with a clear identity? Does it position you as something distinct in your market or playing field? When someone says your name, what do people think? At a party or business function, how are you introduced? When opportunities arise, where are you on the call list? Do colleagues place you in the big sea of sameness with your peers, or do you rise above the rest, into a place of your own with a unique personal brand?

Brand *Moi* is your personal mark that makes you special, memorable, desirable, and worth extra money in the bank. The power of branding creates the perception of leadership and competency in the minds of market. Personal brands start at the core of one's existence and spread throughout every point of contact to your target audience.

Some people contend that personal branding is for conceited egomaniacs, politicians, or rock stars. I contend that people who think like that will be left behind. Think for a moment about someone you really admire. Would he have achieved his same status if he'd lived in a cave and didn't consider the value of exposure? Would she have been invited to participate with other winners in her industry? What if they had never given thought to their personal identity or brand? Would they receive the recognition if they were never strategic about their actions? Probably not.

Personal branding is a smart, powerful tool. Bottom line: It's about being *more* of who you really are. It's simply defining and communicating your purpose, personality, and passions.

People, just like commercial products, have a natural brand—the one we are born with, the one we earn over time. It's the sum of how the market perceives us, our actions, our behavior, and our level of integrity. As we grow up, develop, and set career and life goals, we have a choice. We can "go with the flow," operating in a purely reactive natural brand mode, or we can create a conscious, strategic, personal brand.

Having a Brand *Moi* requires energy, resources, and commitment. Making the choice to work and live your brand will open doors to more opportunities, money, and freedom. In addition, branded people tend to receive stronger support from peers and business associates, which allows them to accomplish more things, conjure more authority, and increase credence for their decisions so they enjoy "top of mind" visibility and status.

Creating Your Own Special Brand

When should you brand yourself? Here are some excellent times to embrace a Brand *Moi* program:

1. After you finished a project and you calculated you were paid about three bucks an hour. (Your compensation stinks.)
2. When you worked your tail off for six months and nobody even noticed. (You're invisible.)
3. When you're sick of your competition getting all the new clients. (Your job is on the line.)
4. When a major change takes place in your life and you're thinking the nut ward would be a nice vacation place. (Your life is falling apart.)

It all starts with up-front planning. Investing time to plan your brand is half the battle, and often it makes the difference between real achievement and anonymity. During up-front planning:

1. Set accountable goals for career and personal life.
2. Define your brand and all its engines (i.e., what gives your brand power and stamina).

3. Research your target markets and competition.
4. Map out a working action plan.
5. Execute with passion and consistency.
6. Monitor and modify as needed.

So where do you want to be? What do you want to do? Do you have your eye on a different position in your company? Do you want to own your own company? Do you want to retire and sail around the world? Run for a political or a trade industry office?

I recommend thinking through both personal and professional goals because, in the best-case scenario, they work hand in hand. Set accountable and specific goals in a present-tense voice. For example:

➤ I am the top producer in my firm.
➤ I am able to work three days a week and double my salary.
➤ I am president of organization XYZ.
➤ I am improving my tennis game to a 4.0 level.

Before delving into your brand plan, do a quick, nonscientific assessment on where your brand stands now.

TATTOO TEST: BRAND *MOI*

Is your personal brand working for you? Find out how you rate on the Brand *Moi* Assessment. Read and answer the following questions, determine the scoring significance, and take the appropriate actions.

	YES	NO
Have you documented your personal and professional short- and long-term goals—with accountable measures?	❏	❏
Do you have an action plan with strategies and tactics to achieve these goals?	❏	❏
Can you clearly describe your target audiences (e.g., using demographics, psychographics)?	❏	❏
Can you clearly describe what differentiates you from your competitors vying for similar goals or operating in your playing field?	❏	❏
Can you define your dream reputation?	❏	❏

	YES	NO
Do you consistently express a visual and language communication style?	❏	❏
Have you addressed a group in the past three months?	❏	❏
Are you comfortable with your presentation skills?	❏	❏
Have you been featured in the media or published or e-published an article in the past three months?	❏	❏
Do you have a current professional photo, bio, and speaker introduction?	❏	❏
Do you keep a victory file of significant achievements, praise letters, and PR clips?	❏	❏
Do you use an e-mail or writing signature with your correspondence?	❏	❏
Do you have a signature token or gift that you reward or recognize people with?	❏	❏
Do you assess your personal brand with peer and target audience feedback?	❏	❏

SIGNIFICANCE

Count how many times you responded with the word "yes" and score your test as follows:

10–14 *(A Landed Brand)*
Congratulations! You are breathing your personal brand. It's established, strong, and working for you. Keep up the great work!

6–9 *(A Baby Brand Ready to Be Born)*
You have the seeds to grow a strong personal brand. Continue nurturing, amp up your commitment, and add some additional branding fuel to your engine.

0–5 *(Barely a Brand)*
You are missing opportunities to expand your success. Your competitors are going to be playing more golf and enjoying themselves and their careers. What are you waiting for?

Even if your score is excellent, it's a prudent idea to complete this chapter, since you may want to adjust or update your brand to increase its power.

How to Tell Your Brand Story

Consider public speaking. Write an article for a trade journal in your industry. Create a token gift that is your signature for clients or rewarding subordinates. Volunteer for something that is indicative of your values system. Whatever you do, be consistent and do it regularly.

If your brand is hip, stay hip. Don't post a tired, dated, bad photo of yourself on your Web site or in your company directory. This is your brand. If you are formal and proper, don't use casual language or slang in your correspondence. Speak and write eloquently. If you are on the cutting edge of technology, don't use a 1960-style typeface in your business correspondence. If you are the cream of the crop in your business, don't use advertising that looks like a bad yellow page ad. Your communication needs to scream your brand. This means *all* points of contact.

What people see, they believe. Audit your graphics and visual presentations. This includes every piece of correspondence that you can control. It also includes your wardrobe, eyeglasses, jewelry, and business accessories. Personal appearance expresses your brand every day. Make sure it's saying what you intend it to say. Never forget that your brand is a result of everything you do—how you act, dress, manage, speak, follow through, work with others, and lead.

I challenge you to go deep into your thinking, explore unknown territory, tap into your greatest self, and have the courage to run with what you find! Connect to your customers' souls. Stand out. Be heard. Make your mark and tout the unique and special being you are! Lead, brand, or get left behind.

BRAND PLANNING WORKOUT

The following questions will help move you through your branding process. Remember, a super-personal brand has a strong, distinct identity. It does not follow the pack of sameness.

WHAT ARE YOUR ACCOUNTABLE CAREER AND PERSONAL GOALS?

Short-term (one year out): _____

Long-term (five years out): _____

    Career: _____

    _____

    Personal: _____

    _____

DEFINE YOUR BRAND *MOI.*

    How do you see yourself? _____

    _____

    What are you most proud of? _____

    _____

    What is your favorite responsibility? _____

    _____

    What are you passionate about? _____

    _____

    What do you do well? _____

    _____

    What do you do not so well? _____

    _____

    What are your values? *(These are just a few.)*

Adventure	Growth
Appreciation	Humor
Community	Material Possessions
Creativity	Money
Fame	Security
Family	Service
Freedom	Spirituality
Generosity	Wisdom

WHAT'S UNIQUE ABOUT YOU?

    Characteristics? _____

    _____

Skills? _____

_____

Talents? _____

_____

Experiences? _____

_____

Name five of your most obvious personality traits.

1. _____

2. _____

3. _____

4. _____

5. _____

Where do you add the most value to groups or relationships? _____

_____

Phrases that pay (taglines): _____

_____

Describe your style and/or visual code: _____

_____

How do others see you? _____

_____

How are you introduced at business and social functions? _____

_____

What's the first thing people think of when they hear your name? __

_____

What do they think you do well? What not so well? _____

_____

What moral principle or value do you most associate with yourself?

_____

How would you describe yourself to others who have never met you?

_____

_____

WHO IS YOUR BUYING MARKET?

Prospects and customers (segment and prioritize them):

Supervisors: _____

Peers: _____

Subordinates: _____

Referral sources: _____

Third-party influencers: _____

Who is vying for your next achievement? _____

Who is selling what you are selling to the marketplace? _____

Within your prospective new-business pool, what are your:

Strong suits? _____

Weaknesses? _____

Within your industry, what are your:

Strong suits? _____

Weaknesses? _____

Within your organization, what are your:

Strong suits? _____

Weaknesses? _____

Sample Brand Plan

Instead of being overwhelmed by a long-term plan, I have found it useful to address my long-term goals annually and then create a quarterly working plan that I update, one month before the next quarter. I use my task list on my e-mail program as a daily "to do" list.

This sample—my plan—is a little heavier on the business side and lighter on the personal side, probably an indication of my brand, or maybe I'm just a little shy about sharing all my personal stuff with thousands of readers. Regardless, this is only a guide. You should include what's important to you in both business and personal realms.

Long-Term Goals

➤ Write a *New York Times* best-seller.
➤ Deliver a keynote at the National Speakers Association (NSA) convention.
➤ Appear on CNN or in *The Wall Street Journal.*
➤ Own a timeshare in a jet.

Short-Term Goals

➤ I am generating ____ in the first quarter.
➤ I am developing a profitable relationship with at least three speakers bureaus.
➤ I am reducing my debt by ____ a month.
➤ I am securing at least two significant national publicity placements.
➤ I am landing a syndicated column or TV segment.
➤ I am maintaining my weight at 135.
➤ I am playing tennis at a 4.0 level by ____.
➤ I am sealing a book deal with a great publisher.
➤ I am presenting a breakout session for an NSA convention.
➤ I am performing at least one paid standup by ———.

Strategies

➤ I am confident and resilient.
➤ I am disciplined.
➤ I am extremely focused on "my brand and building it."
➤ I am not going to get discouraged by bumps in the road.
➤ I am striving for brilliance and balance every day!
➤ I avoid things that do not get me closer to my goals.
➤ I try new things and am fearless and adventuresome.
➤ I am making things happen.
➤ I don't whine or drink too much wine.
➤ I don't hang out with people who do not add positively to my life.

- ➤ I am meeting new people I admire and like being around.
- ➤ I forgive people who disappoint me.
- ➤ I am taking care of my asthma and avoiding secondhand smoke.
- ➤ I am spending time with my mother, sister, her family, and my friends.
- ➤ I am continuing to learn.
- ➤ I shake off stuff I cannot control.

Tactics

- ➤ I plan my week every Sunday and develop a leads list.
- ➤ I plan, prioritize tasks, and sync my Palm daily.
- ➤ I schedule exercise, learning, and downtime daily.
- ➤ I eat a balanced, low-fat diet.
- ➤ I drink eight glasses of water a day.
- ➤ I allow sufficient recovery time for my body and mind.
- ➤ I perform at live mics at least four times a month.
- ➤ I attend two quality network events a week.
- ➤ I update my sales kit and Web site accordingly.
- ➤ I am writing a 300-page book to be completed by ____.
- ➤ I am actively marketing, via the Internet, and posting my content in four target places.
- ➤ I am actively marketing through my database with bimonthly e-mails.
- ➤ I am adding three more products to my selling model.
- ➤ I am updating my video.
- ➤ I send mailings to my speakers bureau list every sixty days.
- ➤ I read industry journals and *The Wall Street Journal* every day.
- ➤ I visit my competitors' Web sites and watch them perform.
- ➤ I schedule and devote ten hours a week to mastering my speaking and comedy.
- ➤ I make contact with ten qualified leads every week.

Sample Redprint

Lifetime Vision

I, Karen Post, am the Branding Diva. I am an internationally known speaker and branding expert who is highly compensated and pursued by top venues, executives, and corporations to make positive things happen, help grow businesses, and make people feel good.

Values

> - I value me.
> - I value my independence.
> - I value financial security.
> - I value my health and appearance.
> - I value the thrill of challenge and risk.
> - I value achievement and recognition.
> - I value beautiful and fine material and natural things.
> - I value my personal relationships, my family, friends, and my advisers.
> - I value creative environments.

Brand Name

Karen Post, The Branding Diva

Brand Promise

I spread the good word of branding and educate and entertain businesses and professionals so they can enrich their lives.

Brand Position

I am a witty, creative, fearless businesswoman who, through living in the trenches of business and marketing, has become a sought-after expert in the area of branding. I coined the term "Brain Tattoo" as a symbol of a successful brand for any size business. I am a street-smart practitioner who lives by the motto, "No limits, no rules, and no excuses." I am entrepreneurial and sometimes get annoyed by conventional wisdom.

Brand Personality

I am a driven businesswoman, optimistic and passionate about my work and tennis game. I am an information sponge and thrive on change and risk. I believe a sense of humor and a positive attitude are the most critical attributes anyone can have. I'm high-energy, intuitive, and quick on my feet and exude a strong visual and aesthetic standard.

Brand Packaging

I have simple, crisp, quality style. Black is my favorite color. In all cases things must be coordinated and current. I have a prestigious address and drive a Porsche. My communication and promotional material is always clean, bold, and little edgy.

Brand Experience

An adventure, always entertaining, and it does not matter if it has not been done before!

Phrases That Pay

➤ "Run like the rest, and you too will be roadkill."
➤ "Brand big or drown fast."
➤ "Lead, brand, or get left behind."

Personal Brain Tattoo Tool Kits

If you are serious about creating a strong personal brand, see if you have your personal Tattoo Tool Kit pulled together. If not, get it together. You may be missing some great opportunities.

Here are two different Tattoo Tool Kits—one for someone employed by a firm, the other for independent or self-employed folks. If you work for a company or organization, you may have some company guidelines for communicating to business, client, or media contacts. However, there are still many opportunities to disseminate your brand message to your targets.

Tool Kit 1: For Individuals Employed by a Company

❑ A professional headshot photo in digital and print format
❑ One paragraph that sums you up professionally
❑ One paragraph that sums you up professionally, with a slice of your personal interests
❑ A one-page bio highlighting your professional achievements and experience
❑ A series of articles on your area of expertise
❑ A victory file of letters and testimonial quotes from your admirers
❑ A file of publicity clips
❑ An e-mail signature that has your contact information and a branding element
❑ Personalized communication materials that adhere to your com-

pany standards (e.g., can be note cards or postcards branded with your essence or a consistent style of purchased cards)

- ❑ A phone message that supports your brand essence
- ❑ A wardrobe that supports your brand style and substance
- ❑ At least one solid speaking presentation related to your business interests
- ❑ A thirty- to sixty-second written introduction about yourself, which can be delivered during your speeches
- ❑ Promotional giveaway items that symbolize your personal brand essence

Tool Kit 2: For the Self-Employed

- ❑ A professional headshot photo in digital and print format
- ❑ Additional professional-quality photos of you in action and representing your brand, in digital and print format
- ❑ One paragraph that sums you up professionally
- ❑ One paragraph that sums you up professionally, with a slice of your personal interests
- ❑ A one-page bio highlighting your professional achievements and experience
- ❑ A series of articles on your area of expertise
- ❑ A victory file of letters and testimonial quotes from your admirers
- ❑ A file of publicity clips
- ❑ An e-mail signature that has your contact information and a branding element
- ❑ Personalized communication materials (e.g., can be note cards or postcards branded with your essence or a consistent style of purchased greeting cards)
- ❑ A phone message that supports your brand essence
- ❑ A wardrobe that supports your brand style and substance
- ❑ At least one solid speaking presentation related to your business interests
- ❑ A thirty- to sixty-second written introduction about yourself, to be delivered during your speeches
- ❑ Promotional giveaway items that symbolize your personal brand essence
- ❑ Advertising that is consistent with your brand image
- ❑ A professional Web site that reflects your brand
- ❑ A professional PowerPoint presentation that reflects your brand

- ❏ A business card that is memorable and relevant and reflects your brand
- ❏ A letterhead package that is memorable and relevant and reflects your brand

In today's competitive world, professionals need an edge to rise to the top of their chosen field. It's a crowded environment with many qualified folks vying for that same place in the sun. Doing up-front planning and being conscious of your desired brand and career goals can make a huge difference in the speed and degree of your success.

Five-Second Brand Bites—You Are Your Own Brand

1. We are *all*, in a sense, "a product." We sell, we pitch, we persuade, and we advocate for stuff that is a part of a greater plan, which will (we hope) fulfill a dream or take us across a finish line.
2. A Brand *Moi* is your personal mark. It symbolizes *who* you are and *what* you stand for, and defines your unique contribution to the world.
3. We can "go with the flow," staying with our natural brand, or we can create a *conscious, strategic, personal* brand.
4. Making the choice to work and live your brand will open doors to more *opportunities, money,* and *freedom* than if you operated in a purely reactive natural brand mode.
5. Your brand is a result of *everything* you do—how you act, dress, manage, speak, follow through, work with others, and lead.

chapter 4

Brand Warriors: Qualities of Great Brand Builders

In 1997, Mike Myers created Austin Powers, International Man of Mystery, as the lead character in the smash movie. Years later, this psychedelic, *mojo*-driven Brit with bad teeth is an ultimate international brand stud. His name is worth a ton and, as Powers, Myers has become an icon of pop culture, his face adorning every kind of merchandise, from flip-flops to stationery.

What did it take to get that brand and every other successful brand on the minds of the market? It's what I call getting in the creative groove—entering a mental zone where leaders soar and are not scared to make mistakes or to travel to unknown places.

These bravo brands, the big ones we all know and buy, are packed with punch. They are managed and led by fearless brand warriors. These folks let their creativity flow and then act on those new ideas!

Creativity

Those who devise truly memorable tattoos are extremely creative. People don't respond to boring, and when they don't respond, they don't buy! The "poor me" branding buffoons, the ones who think their brand point of distinction is their great service, their fine people, or the fact they are a one-stop shop, end up whining all day about their weak brand. Excuse me, that type of thinking and branding is lame, lightweight, and downright pathetic. Customers *expect* those things, and everyone claims them.

Branding is about being noticed, being heard, and standing for something pretty darn cool. Closed minds, sleeping brain cells, and lack of creative thinking and stimuli are dangerous, if not deadly! Ask yourself the following questions, and be brutally honest in your answers.

➤ Is the name of your brand so generic that there are at least four similar-sounding names in your industry or a related industry?

➤ Are your promotional and communication materials ho-hum, boring? Do they have strong similarities to your competitors' in look, feel, and content?

➤ Do you spend good money on bad, boring brochures that yap for days about features and other things your customers don't even care about?

➤ Are your products and services just like your competitors?

➤ Do your PR efforts consist solely of new-hire releases and saying "no comment" when the media calls?

➤ Does your trade show booth fold in a box and include a fish bowl for business cards? Is your business card about as exciting as a phone bill?

➤ Could your ads serve as sleeping medication?

➤ Does your Web site look like a yellow pages ad?

Please tell me it isn't so. If it is, find the paper shredder. This is your wake-up call!

Conformity will eat your lunch. Creativity will land your brand.

It costs organizations more time and money to make an impact on a mind when they sing the same song as everyone else. Buyers get confused and they don't see you or your brand as special. They see you as another dumb commodity. Not good.

Your brand needs to break away from the pack and lose the "me, too" mind-set. This fictional safe zone will just dilute a brand. A Brain Tattoo is special in the minds of the market and is not watered down by streams of sameness. You *can* do this. It just takes a little brand willpower and some creative ways of approaching your business.

I asked creativity expert Michael Michalko, author of the best-selling book *Thinkertoys*, if creativity could be learned. "Yes," he said. "It's a myth that creativity cannot be learned and that you are either born creative or you are not. Creativity is not genetically determined. You can learn to become creative by learning how to become a productive thinker.

"Most people of average intelligence, given data or some problem, can figure out the expected conventional response. Typically, we think reproductively—that is, based on how we handled similar problems encountered in the past. When confronted with problems, we fixate on something in our past that has worked before. We ask, 'What have I been taught in life, education, or work [about] how to solve the problem?' Then we analytically select the most promising approach based on experience, excluding all other approaches, and work within a clearly defined direction toward the solution of the problem. Because of the soundness of the steps based on experience, we become arrogantly certain of the correctness of our conclusion."

Michalko stressed, *"If you always think the way you've always thought, you'll always get what you've always gotten—the same old ideas.* In contrast, creative thinkers think productively, not reproductively. When confronted with a problem, they ask, 'How many different ways can I look at it? How can I rethink the way I see it? How many different ways can I solve it?' instead of 'What have I been taught by someone else about how to solve this problem?' They tend to come up with many different responses, some of which are unconventional and possibly unique.

"With productive thinking, you generate as many alternative approaches as you can. You consider the least obvious as well as the most likely approaches. It is the willingness to explore all approaches that is important, even after you have found a promising one. Einstein was once asked what the difference was between him and the average person. He said that if you asked the average person to find a needle in the haystack, the person would stop when he or she found a needle. He, on the other hand, would tear through the entire haystack looking for all the possible needles.

"So, how do you go from 'not feeling particularly creative' to [being] a 'creative genius'? A growing number of scholars are offering evidence that characterizes the way geniuses think," explained Michalko. "By studying the notebooks, correspondence, conversations, and ideas of the world's greatest thinkers, they have teased out common thinking strategies and styles of thought that enabled geniuses to generate volumes of novel and great ideas."[1]

How Brand Builders Think

The following strategies are common to the thinking styles of creative geniuses in science, art, and industry throughout history:[2]

➤ **Geniuses look at problems in many different ways.** To solve a problem creatively, the thinker must abandon the initial approach that stems from experience and reconceptualize the problem. By not settling for one perspective, geniuses do not merely solve existing problems, like inventing an environmentally friendly fuel; they identify new ones.

➤ **Geniuses make their thoughts visible.** The explosion of creativity during the Renaissance was intimately tied to the recording and conveying of vast knowledge in a parallel language—a language of drawings, graphs, and diagrams. For instance, Galileo revolutionized science by making his thoughts visible with diagrams, maps, and drawings while his contemporaries used conventional mathematical and verbal approaches.

➤ **Geniuses produce.** A distinguishing characteristic of genius is immense productivity. Thomas Edison held 1,093 patents, still the record. He guaranteed productivity by giving himself and his assistants idea quotas. His personal quota was one minor invention every ten days and a major invention every six months. Bach wrote a cantata every week, even when he was sick or exhausted. Mozart produced more than 600 pieces of music. Geniuses produce. Period.

➤ **Geniuses make novel combinations.** Like the highly playful child with a pail full of Legos, a genius is constantly combining and recombining ideas, images, and thoughts into different combinations in her conscious and subconscious mind.

➤ **Geniuses force relationships.** If one particular style of thought stands out about creative genius, it is the ability to make juxtapositions between dissimilar subjects. The facility to connect the unconnected allows them to see things others are blind to. Leonardo da Vinci forced a relationship between the sound of a bell and a stone hitting water, which enabled him to make the connection that sound travels in waves.

➤ **Geniuses think in opposites.** Physicist and philosopher David Bohm believed geniuses were able to think different thoughts because they could tolerate ambivalence between opposites or two incompatible subjects. Thomas Edison's invention of a practical system of lighting involved combining wiring in parallel circuits with high-resistance filaments in his bulbs, two things that were not considered possible by conventional thinkers. In fact, they were not considered at all because of an assumed incompatibility. Because Edison could tolerate the ambivalence between two incompatible things, he could see the relationship that led to his breakthrough.

➤ **Geniuses think metaphorically.** Aristotle considered metaphor a sign of genius, believing that the individual who had the capacity to perceive resemblances between two separate areas of existence and link them together was a person of special gifts. If unlike things are alike in some ways, perhaps they are so in others. Einstein derived and explained many of his abstract principles by drawing analogies with everyday occurrences, such as rowing a boat or standing on a platform while a train passed by.

➤ **Geniuses prepare themselves for chance.** Whenever we attempt to do something and fail, we end up doing something else. As simplistic as this statement may seem, it is the first principle of creative accident. We may ask ourselves why we have failed to do what we intended, and this is the reasonable, expected thing to do. But the creative accident provokes a different question: What have we done? Answering that question in a novel, unexpected way is the essential creative act. It is not luck, but creative insight of the highest order. Too many people fail to answer opportunity's knock at the door because they have to finish some preconceived plan. Creative geniuses do not wait for the gifts of chance; instead, they actively seek the accidental discovery.

Recognizing the common thinking strategies of creative geniuses and applying them will make you more creative in your work and personal life. Creative geniuses are geniuses because they know "how" to think instead of "what" to think.

Brain Tattooing is your opportunity to tell your story, keep your promise, and stand for something remarkable. To do this, you must open your mind to vast-reaching and new possibilities in all parts of your brand. This includes, but of course is not limited to, your product, your name, your promotion, your positioning and point of difference, your distribution channels, and your packaging.

Consider for a moment these creative geniuses. Chester Carlson invented xerography in 1938. Virtually every major corporation, including IBM and Kodak, scoffed at his idea and turned down his offer to produce copying machines. They claimed that since carbon paper was cheap and plentiful, who in his right mind would buy an expensive copier?

Fred Smith, while a student at Yale, came up with the concept of Federal Express, a national overnight-delivery service. The U.S. Postal

Service, UPS, his own business professor, and virtually every delivery expert in the United States predicted failure for such an enterprise. According to their experiences in the industry, no one, they said, will pay a fancy price for speed and reliability.

Creativity Workout

Michael Michalko suggests pumping up your mind. Like building a new muscle in the gym, the more you exercise your mind using these techniques, the stronger your creativity is. Following each "rep" (i.e., step or exercise) are specific ideas that can open up a big brand storm of new opportunities.

1. **Set an idea quota.** Give your mind a workout. Set yourself an idea quota for a challenge you are working on, such as generating five new ideas every day for a week. Charge yourself with the task of coming up with five new ways to:
   - ➤ Touch your customer.
   - ➤ Make doing business with you easier.
   - ➤ Promote your point of difference.
   - ➤ Improve your Web site's friendliness.
   - ➤ Add value to your offering.
2. **Get tone.** Fighter pilots say "I've got tone" when their radar locks onto a target. That's the point at which the pilot is totally focused on the target. "Getting tone" in branding means paying attention to what's happening around you; for example:
   - ➤ Your customers' gripes and their praises
   - ➤ What your competition is doing
   - ➤ What the media is saying
3. **Don't be a "Duke of Habit."** Dukes of Habit must always do things the same way, must have everything in its place, and are lost if someone violates their routine. Dukes of Habit are limited problem-solvers. Don't be one. Make it a point to change:
   - ➤ The route you take to work
   - ➤ The people you eat lunch with
   - ➤ The order of your day
   - ➤ What newspapers you read
4. **Feed your head.** Creative thinkers read to feed their minds new information and ideas. As Gore Vidal put it, "The brain that doesn't feed itself eats itself." Don't stop with reading. Be an information sponge—listen, watch, and ask questions. To feed your head:

- Go to a children's movie.
- Visit an obscure art gallery.
- Try a month of comedy—visit a club, see a movie, or read a funny book.
- Experience a new ethnic experience—dine somewhere new.

5. **Do a content analysis.** Scan the world around you. Actively observe popular culture. Spot trends in ads. Listen to different radio stations. Drive around in different markets. Attend lectures, conference, and seminars. Check out some different learning resources: Read *Brandweek, American Demographics, mental-floss,* or vintage business magazines. Hang out at the bus terminal or airport. Attend an out-of-town advertising federation award's event.

6. **Build a brain bank.** Collect and store ideas like a pack rat. Keep a container of random or interesting ideas, ads, photos, words, articles, and designs. When you need a new idea, shake up the container and pick one. One great idea can trigger the next. Keep junk mail, magazines, cool ads, bad ads, catalogs, and interesting business cards.

7. **Be a travel junkie.** Whenever you are feeling stale and bored, go somewhere new—a store, the library, a museum, or a toy shop. Wander around with an open brain; check out new things. Your mind is like vegetation. It will flourish in one soil and droop in another. Go to the circus, the zoo, garage sales, estate sales, and festivals.

8. **Capture your thoughts.** Ralph Waldo Emerson once wrote, "Look sharply after your thoughts. They come unlooked for, like a new bird seen in your trees, and if you turn to your usual task, disappear." You have to record your ideas, in your personal digital assistant or on a writing pad. Don't forget:
   - Problems
   - Stressors
   - Snappy names
   - Companies to co-brand with
   - Events

9. **Think right.** Consciously work to make your thinking more fluent and flexible (fluency means number of ideas; flexibility means creativity). Making a list is a powerful way to increase your thinking fluency because it forces you to focus your energy in a very productive way.

10. **Keep an idea log.** The idea log is one of the CIA's favorite techniques for recording information. There is a written log for each problem, which is used to record ideas, facts, thoughts, questions,

and so on. This way the agent can focus instantly on the ideas, comparisons, interrelationships, and data relating to a given problem. Maintain an idea log. Each section could be devoted to separate aspects of your business and personal life. Sections can include:

➤ Business leads
➤ New resources
➤ People doing awesome things
➤ Alternative media
➤ PR stunts
➤ Clever headlines
➤ Free stuff and cool offers
➤ Stuff you can't afford

Freethinking, creativity, and innovation make the world go round. Take a huge step from brand bland to brand brilliance by unleashing your mind to "big idea nirvana." Whatever business or industry you are in, there are endless, untapped ways in which you can benefit from your brand, breathe it into your balance sheet, and enjoy total brand bliss.

Don't go to the "been there, done that" file in your head. That's where your competitors migrate. Go where the majority fears to go, where there is uncertainty, and where the next home run is discussed as a horrific problem.[3]

FROM THE BRAIN TRUST

Creativity

"Creativity represents a miraculous coming together of the uninhibited energy of the child with its apparent opposite and enemy—the sense of order imposed on the disciplined adult intelligence."
—NORMAN PODHORETZ, *author, editor, and senior fellow at the Hudson Institute*

Now that your list of new, fresh ideas is flowing over, you've got to do something with them. I never said branding was a no-work proposition. This is where the real fun begins.

Fearlessness

Branding is not for followers. Followers are just another commodity.

The heart of a great brand is its point of difference in the category and its place in the minds of the market. While many businesses claim to believe in the brand spirit, they fall short when it comes to the courage to be a unique, distinct brand. No matter what business sector you are in, I guarantee on any given day you can pick up a trade journal or an ad or visit a Web site and if you cover up the brand name, you will not have any idea who is selling what. It all looks the same.

If you want to stick your brand where it counts—land it on the cranium of your buyers—you've got to have courage to try something new, different, and bold, not boring and mundane. I have seen these sins of sameness committed in all businesses. This fear of breaking the norm, the dread of being different, and the thought of being talked about—most companies could use a little industry chatter about their brands.

No Risk, No Brand

For your operation to land a big one and create a true Brain Tattoo, you must know that leaving your comfort zone is required. For some, this brand spark starts with the innovation in their product or service: They buck the system. For others, it's their method of delivery: They break the rules. And for some others it's the packaging of their brand that makes them a true pioneer.

Resistance is a given on the journey to a successful Brain Tattoo. Remember that most businesses play by a common set of rules. They follow the pack. They are afraid to step out of the safe space. This is not where you will find great brands growing. This is where you will find commodities fighting for the tiniest slice in their category.

Vision—Clear and Simple

Many human brains have limited storage and recall capacity. Big brands are simple brands.

As you break ground on trying something a little risky concerning your brand, it's natural to start enjoying a new flow of creative, daring, and sometimes darn right wacky ideas. This is a beautiful thing. However, the by-product of these newfound, freewheeling thoughts sometimes brings an overload of options, creating severe brand message muddiness.

Don't fall in love with every idea. It will cause brand death. Boil your message down so that Joe Six-Pack or a five-year-old kid gets it. Decide on a single brand direction or story and stick with it. The human mind can take only so much. Your buyer's mental capacity is probably already peaking. Decisiveness on your brand in the early stages will pay big rewards in your branding journey.

A singular message brand is cost-efficient to communicate and much easier to Brain Tattoo on your buyer's mind than multiple messages. If you can't sort out the myriad brilliant ideas, consider spinning off a couple of brands with strong relevance and clear benefit to a target audience. If that's not an option, store them in your idea log for a later time.

Strategic Thinking

Branding is not *just* a marketing issue. Branding is an intricate part of all business functions. It is not the exclusive domain of the marketing department or your ad agency. Finance, operations, human resources, and technology strategies need to reflect your brand's values and support your brand story. Without this cohesive harmony and across-the-board departmental buy-in, a brand faces a more expensive uphill battle to success.

Commitment

Branding is not a quick fix to a sales problem. Branding can certainly make the sales process easier, but it's not a magic wand. Building a business today brings short-term pressures from shareholders and financial partners to be hugely profitable—fast. Unfortunately, this stress sometimes causes business leaders to focus on only immediate tactics rather than longer-term strategic initiatives.

Successful branding does not happen overnight. It is a sustained investment in which value accumulates. I don't mean twenty years. Meeting your brand's milestones and scheduling depends on your specific business goals and the market factors in your category. I just hate to see good ideas junked too soon because the marketing department got bored or the CEO became impatient.

Although technology has certain sped up the ability to brand faster and get your story out to a large targeted audience, brand leaders still need to stay committed to the program for an ample time before they ditch a sound strategy. Brand leaders are also flexible and adjust to market shifts. They keep a brand fresh and relevant while maintaining and being true to who they are.

Behind every super-brand is a super-brand leader. The behavior of these leaders, which leads to their success, can be learned.

The Ideal Mix: Smart Research, an Intuitive Gut, and Perfect Timing

You have now arrived at the $50 million question: Is a monumental research program always necessary and a ticket to a home-run brand?

Marty Neumeier, brand consultant and author of *The Brand Gap*, noted that there has been an aversion to research in the boardrooms of some of the world's most innovative brands. Sony founder Akio Morita believed that testing new ideas was folly. "Our plan is to lead the public," he said. "They do not know what is possible." Even back in the command-and-control days of the production line, Henry Ford's decision to manufacture automobiles was driven by intuition rather than market research. "If we had asked the public what they wanted," he explained, "they would have said 'faster horses.'"

Neumeier goes on to say, "Innovators often feel that using research is like trying to chart the future in a rearview mirror. They've seen too many products and messages aimed where the audience was last sighted, instead of where it's likely to be tomorrow." Creativity is subjective, but only until it reaches the marketplace—then it's measurable. Ford's and Sony's innovations certainly were measured, not by research but by the market itself.[4]

Other significant brand owners, however, do not make a move without validation, confirmation, and spending shiploads on studies.

As a card-carrying right-brain intuitive and an often off-the-planet thinker dealing with both big-budget and no-budget brands, I've found a strong pattern of success with the mix of these two opposing philosophies.

Smart Research

Ask the right questions, of the right folks, in the correct forum, and make sure you have sensible (i.e., realistic) expectations.

➤ **Focus Groups.** Understand that a small group of individuals in a one-time focus study will not garner quantitative findings. Focus studies are best for exploratory research, eliciting needs, uncovering emotional issues, and spanning creative concepts. This type of research is qualitative. It tells us "why" but not "how many" (which would be quantitative).

➤ **Personal Interviews.** Personal interviews can be qualitative and quantitative if your pool is large enough. A skilled, unbiased interviewer can make the difference in the degree of quality data on preferences, attitudes, and needs.

➤ **Telephone Surveys.** Telephone interviews can be qualitative and quantitative if your pool is large enough. The more structured they are, the better. Offering a reward sometimes will encourage respondents to spend more time on the phone.

➤ **Mail Surveys.** Mail surveys are quantitative, use highly structured questionnaires, and work best when preceded by an exploratory focus study.

➤ **Web Surveys.** Web surveys are quantitative. They can provide faster turnaround than other forms of research and real-time results can be made available. Current limitations are that the online population is still somewhat younger and wealthier than the average population.

Choose the Method That Best Fits Your Needs and Budget. A single method or a combination of several methods can provide useful information on brand awareness; product usage; customer satisfaction; and employee, vendor, and public market attitudes, behavior, and needs. Many times this research can be achieved in-house and without spending a lot of money. Adding a professional research firm or consultant will add cost; however, if you can afford it, the investment may be worth it because of the quality and timeliness of the data received.

In addition to gathering primary buyer data, it's often a viable investment to purchase a syndicated market study. These studies take a snapshot of an industry and often supply market opportunities and demographic data for a reasonable fee. Many large research firms conduct studies of this nature on behalf of trade industries. FIND/SVP (www .findsvp.com) in New York offers more than forty studies spanning consumer goods to technology.

Should research be the Holy Grail in all your decisions? Absolutely not. Just ask The Coca-Cola Company. It spent more than $4 million testing New Coke against Pepsi. The beverage won that battle, but failed miserably in the market. In hindsight, many believe disregard for the emotional connection and brand loyalty associated with Coke affected the testing design and conclusions.

In addition to these common avenues of gathering intelligence and data, new techniques, methodologies, and research products continue to evolve. Many are excellent research options for both developing new brands and sustaining established ones. The following are noteworthy tools to consider:

QualiQuant Studies (B2B and Consumer Products). Rodney Kayton, managing partner of Schwartz Research (www.schwartzresearch .com) in Tampa, Florida, created the QualiQuant study. This proprietary process is a multidimensional technique combining qualitative and quantitative methods to extrapolate both hard data and emotional response. Ideal for branding campaigns, it is cost-effective and can be conducted on a short turnaround. Respondents are exposed to assorted marketing materials including TV spots, print advertisements, and marketing collaterals. This research methodology consistently generates rich discussion about perceptions and levels of acceptance and can determine why choices are made. Specific study objectives can include market awareness (yours and/or competitors), brand name associations, marketing language idea elicitation, advertising, and/or creative concepts idea elicitation, packaging idea elicitation, and promotional offer idea elicitation.

Opt-In Respondent Panel (B2B and Consumer Products). Clickin Research (www.clickinresearch.com) in Austin, Texas, developed the Cyberleague, an opt-in respondent panel. Now a panel of more than 100,000 people, its extensive profiling allows targeted selection of highly specific samples for custom and syndicated studies. The Cyberleague can be segmented for specified demographic, psychographic, activity-based, or geographic requirements. It uses a profiling database that includes media, computer, Internet use, family and leisure activities, and shopping patterns. The Cyberleague includes men, women, and kids over twelve years old. Some examples of psychographic segments are:

- Business owners
- Cable, satellite, and TV service subscribers
- Chief information and technology officers
- Educators and students
- Gamblers
- Gamers
- Home remodelers
- Information technology workers
- Investors
- Outdoor enthusiasts
- Specialty beverage drinkers
- Tech product owners
- Teens and their parents
- Business and leisure travelers

Big Business Research for Smaller Companies (Consumer Products). When someone says ACNielsen (www.acnielsen.com), most think Fortune 500 companies. While Nielsen is the world leader in consumer research, it also has a service group geared toward small and medium-size manufacturers. The Select-800 group works specifically with new or start-up brands. Understanding the unique needs of a growing business, it educates management on the information and methods that can deliver on your needs and budget. Services include:

- Scantrack retail measurement
- Homescan consumer panel
- Account-level information
- Retail account reports
- Sample trading areas
- Census trading areas
- Chain-buying points
- Package, flavor, and product trends

Brand Equity Measurement System (Consumer Products). ACNielsen has also developed a brand equity measurement system called Winning B®ands. It allows a business to manage, monitor, and improve a brand's health. Developed in consultation with Professor Kevin Keller and John Roberts, world leaders on brand equity thinking, it measures the impact that marketing activity has on current performance and the potential for future performance. In addition, it monitors the impact of competitive activity, diagnoses brand health, and identifies new opportunities for and threats to your brand. Winning B®ands is a modular service, allowing you to focus on advertising activity alone or on a wider range of influences, such as promotions and sponsorship.

Premarket Consumer Insight (Consumer Products). Considering a new brand? ACNielsen's BASES combines primary consumer research with state-of-the-art forecasting techniques to estimate the sales potential of new product initiatives before market entry. It uses proprietary research tools to give clients answers to questions such as:

> ➤ What is the volume potential for my new product?
> ➤ How will a line extension affect my overall brand franchise?
> ➤ How can I improve the productivity of my marketing plan?
> ➤ Who will be the core users of my new product?
> ➤ At what price will I maximize revenue or profit potential for my new brand?
> ➤ How will my competitor's new product launch affect my brand?

Ethnography, Reality-Based Research. For hundreds of years, anthropologists have studied natives and their cultures in foreign lands. Today, a new breed of researchers studies consumers in their living environments. Through the practice of ethnography, research teams immerse, participate, observe, and take part in ongoing informal dialogue to uncover insights to transform businesses and their brands.

While most qualitative research techniques provide the memory of the experience, ethnography offers the product experience as it happens: on the consumer's own turf, untainted by faulty recollection, peer pressure, or an unfamiliar environment. Two leaders in this area are Housecalls, Inc. (www.housecallsobserve.com) on the East Coast and, on the West Coast, Gestalt Consumer Ethnography (www.gestaltgroup.com).

All of these research vehicles have merit. However, bear in mind that while being an information sponge can be a good thing, being a prisoner to research—or hiring a scaredy-cat manager who is not willing to move an inch without a research security blanket—can be a costly mistake.

An Intuitive Gut

Sometimes the hunches just have it. Instinctive knowledge without the use of rational processes is frightening to many. From my experience, I have to tell you, don't disregard your gut instinct, especially if it has worked for you in the past.

If a product that bombs won't kill your business and you've got other revenue streams, the money you spend on a launch is the greatest research you can do, and it takes your product to the people, the ultimate test.

Perfect Timing

The next time you're feeling sorry for yourself about some big company's fat budget, just remind yourself of your greatest entrepreneurial power—the ability to make something fabulous happen fast, without bureaucracy and wretched committees. Timing is everything, and that may be an understatement. The most comprehensive research study in the world won't mean squat if you miss the window of a timely brand opportunity.

Five-Second Brand Bites—What Every Brand Warrior Must Know

1. People don't respond to boring, and when they don't respond they don't buy! Conformity will eat your lunch. Creativity will *land your brand.*
2. Brand warriors are *creative* and *fearless,* and stay *committed* to the cause.
3. Brand warriors have a *clear, singular vision* and a *global view,* but they are also *flexible* and adjust to market shifts.
4. *Invest* in the up-front time. It will pay off. *Involve* your staff and others whose opinions you respect. Do the research, but don't ignore your intuition, and remember that timing counts.

End Notes

1. Michael Michalko, "A Theory About Genius," 1991 (available at http://www.creativethinking.net/CreativeThinkingArchive.htm). Used by permission of the author.

2. Ibid. Used by permission of the author.
3. Michael Michalko, *Thinkertoys* (Berkeley, Calif.: Ten Speed Press, 1991), pp. 1221. Used by permission of the author.
4. Marty Neumeier, *The Brand Gap* (Indianapolis, Ind.: New Riders/ AIGA, 2003). Used by permission of the author.

chapter 5

Branding Basics: How to Construct Your Tattoo Plan

Whether you have an existing brand, and just tested its potency with the Tattoo Test, or you are birthing a new brand, the next phase is vital. A brand with no plan is like a winning lottery ticket you can't find.

Your tattoo plan is critical to landing a brand. Working from a thought-out document will keep your brand ambassadors on track, help you see new opportunities, and provide a benchmark for measuring your brand's success. The sooner you get started, the sooner your markets will be sporting one of those desired and permanent Brain Tattoos on their minds.

The degree and detail of your plan may depend on your volume, resources, and staff. Page count of your plan is not half as important as covering your brand plan basics. This chapter outlines a simple questioning process that is a good starting point for any branding plan.

Management guru and brand builder (who hasn't heard of *The 7 Habits of Highly Effective People*?) Stephen Covey says it so well: "Always start with the end in mind." This certainly applies to brand building. Think of marketing as your process and the brand as the end-result.

Picture the perfect brand. At the beginning of your brand planning process, visualize the dream brand for your product, your service, or yourself. What does it look like, sound like, and feel like?

Ask yourself the following important questions about your business and your ultimate brands. If your situation is a start-up brand, you may not be able to answer the last few questions yet. If you are an existing brand, all of the questions are important and should be answered.

Questions to Ask Before You Begin Your Plan

Invest the time up-front, because it will pay off. Do not just whip through these questions in a few minutes over your favorite beverage. Take your time; involve your staff or other people whose opinions you respect. The answers to these questions will drive the development of your working tattoo plan.

ABOUT YOUR MARKET

Describe your buying market: _____

Size in potential sales: _____

How much of the market do you presently own? _____

Challenges and changes (consider industry, economic, technology, competitors, weather, terrorism, etc.): _____

Opportunities (consider industry, economic, technology, and competitors): _____

What future trends could affect your market and how? _____

ABOUT YOUR CATEGORY

Whether you are joining a market category or creating a new one, describe your category: _____

ABOUT YOUR TARGET

Who is your primary target audience? _____

Who is the buyer for this brand with the highest propensity to bring in the best margins and highest total sales? _____

Prioritize your best to worst customer profile:

Demographic profile: _____

Psychographic profile: _____

What is the average sale amount? _____

What is the cost of customer acquisition? _____

What is the life span of a customer? _____

Do you track and use data from current sales? _____

Who are the influencers? _____

ABOUT BRAND CHANNELS

What is the strongest channel for revenue from your target? (Prioritize from the following.)

- ❑ Selling to retailers
- ❑ Selling direct to buyers
- ❑ Selling nonretail business-to-business (B2B)
- ❑ Selling online
- ❑ Exporting
- ❑ Selling by mail order/catalog
- ❑ Selling by infomercials
- ❑ Selling by advertorials
- ❑ Selling by direct response
- ❑ Franchising
- ❑ Selling through networks (multilevel)
- ❑ Selling through affiliate programs
- ❑ Licensing

Do any other channels have strong potential? _____

ABOUT BRAND PRICING

How will your brand be priced compared to the competition? What will this price say to the market? _____
_____
_____

ABOUT YOUR COMPETITORS

To answer the following questions, look at direct competitors and those who are vying for a sale that could tap into your market's purchasing pie.

Name your top-five brand competitors, gross sales on the brand, and amount of their market share.

1. _____
2. _____
3. _____
4. _____
5. _____

Define their brand: _____

Strengths: _____

Weaknesses: _____

Promotional/advertising highlights: _____

Brand personality: _____

Brand promise: _____

Brand phrases that pay: _____

Brand visual code: _____

ABOUT YOUR BRAND

What are your accountable goals? _____

Market share? _____

Sales? _____

Visibility/mind share? _____

Shareholder value? _____

Other goals? _____

What do you believe your current brand says about:

Your purpose? _____

What you do well? _____

What you do not so well? _____

The personality of your brand? _____

What is your brand name? Does it need to be changed? _____

What's unique about your brand?

Visual? _____

Position? _____

Characteristics? _____

Offering? _____

Attributes? _____

What is your promise? _____

If you are an existing brand, do you have phrases that pay?

Taglines (external, internal): _____

Statement of being: _____

If you are an existing brand, do you have a prevalent look and feel or visual code?

Color system: _____

Typefaces: _____

Photo or art style: _____

Graphic pattern or theme: _____

ABOUT OUTSIDE BRAND PROMOTION

What avenues most effectively reach your market? (Choose from the following.)

- ❑ Print
- ❑ Broadcast
- ❑ Cable, network, films, infomercials
- ❑ Radio
- ❑ Direct mail
- ❑ Loyalty programs
- ❑ Customer contact points
- ❑ Brand promo events
- ❑ Cause marketing
- ❑ Publicity
- ❑ Internet
- ❑ Publications
- ❑ Collateral
- ❑ Business cards
- ❑ Airspace (e.g., blimps, airplane streamers)
- ❑ Signage/outdoor/murals
- ❑ Sampling
- ❑ Buzz (word-of-mouth) marketing

What's new in media and avenues to reach your market? _____
_____

ABOUT INTERNAL BRAND PROMOTION

What avenues most effectively reach your troops? (Choose from the following.)

- ❑ Training
- ❑ Reward programs
- ❑ Films
- ❑ Brand promo events
- ❑ Cause marketing
- ❑ Intranet
- ❑ Internal publications
- ❑ Internal collateral
- ❑ Signage/outdoor/murals
- ❑ Sampling/discount program
- ❑ Buzz (word-of-mouth) marketing

ABOUT MARKET PERCEPTIONS OF YOUR BRAND

For the following questions, ask an outside party for input and perspectives:

What is your purpose? _____

What do you do well? _____

What do you not do well? _____

What is the personality of your brand? _____

What is your brand name? _____

What's unique about your brand?

    Visual? _____

    Position? _____

    Characteristics? _____

    Offering? _____

    Attributes? _____

What is your promise? _____

If you were able to answer all of these questions, you should be set to move forward to create a written, working brand document. Remember, great brand plans are flexible and always evolving. If you were unable to answer all the questions, you may need to do additional research before proceeding. I recommend you continue reading the book to the end and then return to the next section to develop your Tattoo Plan.

TATTOO PLAN OUTLINE

Goals (vision, revenues, market share, and profits): _____
_____

Objectives (acquisitions, tangible and intangible milestones): _____
_____

Primary and secondary target markets (demographic and psychographic): _____

Specific strategies for each market (behaviors):_____

Note: Strategies are about behavioral changes. They may cover product, distribution channels, pricing, sales, loyalty, communication, and promotion plans.

Specific tactics for each market (tasks): _____

Note: Tactics are tasks for achieving strategies. Examples are research; packaging; creation of collateral materials; training; advertising; sales; public relations (media, industry, government, employee); grass-roots, online, or direct efforts; events; and merchandising.

Timelines (scheduling): _____

Prime movers (who will do what? in-house vs. outsourced?): _____

Budget (internal and external): _____

Measurement (how will you know the plan is working?): _____

Note: Consider assessing employee turnover, new super-talent recruits, sales, media coverage, profits, stock price, industry recognition, awards, public opinion, or customer and vendor surveys.

Once your Tattoo Plan is complete, it is time to boil everything down and summarize your strongest branding drivers onto a Redprint. This simple form should be introduced to and signed off by your entire staff as part of their orientation, training, or brand powwows. (Note: I recommend including a brand oath. This official format reminds the brand ambassadors of their commitment to the cause and is a symbol of their organizational integrity.)

BRAND REDPRINT

Date: _____

Brand Name: _____

Brand Category (purpose): _____

Unique Brand Distinction: _____

Brand Promise: _____

Brand Personality: _____

Brand Visual Code: _____

Phrases That Pay: _____

Brand Story (no more than fifty words): _____
_____
_____

Brand Oath: _____

As a proud brand builder and co-owner of our great brand, I will always value our brand and do everything in my power to keep our brand landed in the minds, hearts, and souls of our customers, prospects, shareholders, employees, market analysts, and media. I will fight for our brand, respect our brand, and consider it in all-important decisions about our organization.

Brand Builder _____ Date_____

Brand Leader _____ Date_____

Once the Tattoo Plan and Redprint are complete, many companies will go a step further and create a comprehensive brand standards guide or brand book that's made available on their company intranet, in a staff manual, or on a CD. Some companies even test employees on their brand knowledge and graciously reward their commitment to the brand.

Five-Second Brand Bites—Before You Begin

1. A brand with no plan is like a winning lottery ticket you can't find.
2. The degree and detail of your plan may depend on your volume, resources, and staff. Page count is not half as important as covering your brand plan basics.
3. *Always* start with the end in mind.
4. *Visualize* the dream brand at the beginning of your brand planning process.
5. *Invest* the time up-front. It will pay off. *Involve* your staff and others whose opinions you respect.

chapter 6

Brand Naming: Art, Skill, and Luck

At the end of the day, a brand name is "the master art" of the Brain Tattoo: the letters, the sound, the recall, the distinctive nomenclature. Branding experts around the world continually debate the magic formula for creating the best brand names.

Although brand naming is one of the most critical aspects of building a brand, a brand cannot survive on its name alone. The brand name and how the brand is executed are equally vital for a successful and sustained brand life. A great brand name can serve as the anchor to your cause, a symbol for your story, a point of difference in your marketplace, or a memory trigger—in other words, it is just one important part of your branding arsenal.

The task of developing that killer name has become quite complex. For years, business owners and management named their offspring, then creative service firms and ad agencies (often sprinkled by college talent) jumped in, and then the public added its wisdom, often through naming contests. No doubt, each of these sources has produced its share of brilliant as well as very scary names. Now this art, science, skill, and luck service has gone professional. Naming brands is big business and can come with a big price tag. Hire a professional naming company and expect a bill of $10,000 to $100,000 or more *before* the graphic execution or production.

How Much Is a Name Worth?

A great name is worth a great deal. Think about it: If your brand is properly nourished, grows, and has a long shelf life or history—do the math.

Brand Name	Worth
Pentium	$100,000 (estimate)
DreamWorks	$350,000
Internet Explorer	$5 million (includes settlement fee Microsoft paid for use of name)
Netscape	$100,000 (estimate)
Apple Computer	More than $43 million (including fee paid to Apple Records, owned by the Beatles, when the Mac added sound)

You can find these and others on Nametrade.com, a naming resource site that's part of Cintara, a California-based brand and naming consultancy group.

Not all great brand names cost a lot. Nike is one of the best examples. "Nike" is the name of the Greek goddess of victory. The name came in a dream to Jeff Johnson, Nike's first "real" employee, and replaced the company's original name, Blue Ribbon Sports. The company paid Carolyn Davidson, a graphic design student at Portland State University, $35 in 1971 to design the trademark "swoosh."[1]

Finding the Right Name

When faced with the challenge of naming, start with your and your staff's ideas. No matter what names you come up with—even if they are bad—it's a good creative exercise that will help you define (if only for yourself) your brand's essence. If you have the budget, outside input and other naming solutions can also be a very valid investment. Remember, the life and benefit of your brand name may last for years. It's going to be plastered on lots of things, including your market's mind. Whatever you spend, divide it by the projected years of use and value. This same formula applies for investments in corporate identities and taglines. They are as valuable as a great employee or piece of manufacturing equipment.

Should you decide to engage a firm (either a naming consultant or agency), I recommend interviewing at least three. Don't rely on an RFP that's price-driven, but set up personal meetings to assess working style and how each firm views the naming process and *a great brand name*. Certainly, budget is an issue, but it should not be the determining factor. Ask about the following:

> ➤ Past work they have created and sold to clients
> ➤ Their approach, development methods, and pricing
> ➤ Deliverables, including testing, legal searching, and the number of names they will present for the agreed-on price

Ten Questions to Ask Yourself Before You Begin

As in any industry, there are both excellent and poor resources. Consider the working chemistry between you and the project team, the investment needed versus your market opportunity, and the company's past work product. Whether you decide to outsource or create a name on your own, ask yourself the following questions:

1. Who will ultimately decide the name? One person or a team? Whoever that is should be involved in the criteria-building process.
2. What kind of brand are you naming—a company, consumer product, business service, or event?
3. What is the expected life of the brand name?
4. Does the name fit into a larger family of names?
5. Will the brand name be used only in the United States, or will it go global? Remember, today global can mean "on the Internet."
6. Who is your primary audience for the brand names?
7. Are you creating a new category or joining an existing one?
8. If joining a category, what are your competitors' names?
9. What is the essence of your brand—its purpose, promise, personality, position?
10. What are your primary strategies for building your brand?

Once you've established your basic criteria or framework, you can proceed with the grueling task of a name dump of endless possibilities.

Literal and Descriptive vs. Obscure and Emotional

I tend toward obscure and certainly emotional names, primarily because I'm a strong proponent of distinct brands. However, I also believe each case is unique. Sometimes brand names are passed down, and changing them would take an act of Congress. Your answers to the ten questions will help you figure out what is best for your brand. Consider the category, brand positioning, ownership, execution plans, and budget in your decision.

An obscure or unfamiliar word can be a brand home run. Consider Apple, Nike, Google, FUBU, and Yahoo! They all have visibility/frequency, brand storytelling communication, and brand performance. They are all hugely successful brands, although all started as small companies.

Literal and descriptive words can work in some situations. Generally, proceed with caution because these types of names can be more easily copied or imitated, leading to buyer confusion, which usually defeats the purpose of a sound brand.

If you have a big branding budget, you often can sustain a boring, generic, or literal brand name with some other compelling messaging. Take, for example, Southwest Airlines. Its consistently creative and "on brand" advertising has transformed an ordinary, unexciting name into a great brand name. However, most companies don't have the luxury of Southwest's media budget or have not found the right advertising approach to achieve that kind of success.

My advice: Unless you have a big, endless budget, avoid generic names such as Computer Solutions, Performance Printing, or Innovative Technologies. Such names will just make you spend more and work harder at building a brand. In most cases, they simply don't have legs and will likely drown in the sea of sameness. Avoiding generic names is also critical in consumer-packaged products, especially when private label copycats by mass retailers are showing up. Many times the name can be the strong point of difference.

Names to Avoid

Copycat names or names that sound like a competitor or some other big brand are not worth much. Neither are names that are hard to spell or pronounce. Great brand names are:

> ➤ Emotional (they make you feel good and generate curiosity)
> ➤ Memorable (either because they include a compelling sound

or have eye appeal; in essence, they offer crisp and distinct qualities)

➤ Personable (they express a set of human-like traits and exude attitude and style)

➤ Deep (they can be leveraged in promotional, ad, PR, and communication programs)

Sources of Names

Brand names are derived in a variety of ways. Nametrade.com has compiled an excellent summary of many popular practices.

Brand Name Derivations[2]

Style	Example
Abbreviation	FedEx, Raychem, Microsoft
Acronym	UPS, KFC, BP, IBM, TCBY, AOL
Alliteration	Dunkin' Donuts, Roto-Rooter, Planters Peanuts
Allusion/Evocation/Suggestion	London Fog, V-8, KitchenAid
Analogy	Kool-Aid, Amtrak, Gateway 2000
Appropriation	Java, Colt, Dart, Poppy, Barracuda
Arbitrary	Apple, Marimba, Red Pepper, Poppy
Classical Roots	Pentium, Quattro, Avis
Combination/Semantics	Studebagels, NutraSweet, Kodak, Qualcomm
Composition	LaserJet, PowerBook, PageMaker, ImageWriter
Description	Bed, Bath & Beyond; Airbus; Caterpillar
Foreign Language	Fuego Technology, Volare, Montero
Founders	Hewlett-Packard, Hilton, Disneyland, Ford
Historical/Geographical	Winnebago, Rocky Mountain Chocolate Factory
Humor	Cracker Jack, Yahoo!
Metonymy (use of a name or concept for another related one)	Silicon Alley, Starbucks
Mimetics (alternative spelling)	Krispy Kreme, Krazy Glue, Kwik Kopy, Kleenex
Mythological	Centaur, Midas Mufflers, Mercury
Onomatopoeia (imitating sounds associated with the name)	ZapMail, Sizzler Steakhouse, Kookooroo, Kisses
Oxymoron	True Lies, Steel Magnolias, Intimate Strangers

Poetics	Rockin' Tacos, El Pollo Loco, Domino's
Rhyme	Shake 'n Bake, Lean Cuisine, OshKosh B'Gosh
Song or Story Association	Chimney with Care, Orient Express
Sound Symbolism	Talon, Kraft, RoundUp
Symbolism	Tahoe, Yukon, Ford Explorer, Mustang
Truncation	Intel, Intuit, Cisco Systems

Whatever route you take—working with a naming company or a creative consultant, rallying your troops and making it an internal company project, enlisting strangers in a naming contest, or combining several of these methods—you have created an extensive list of possible contenders. Now what?

A Name That Sticks

"Generic names are fine as long as you have a unique product that is unequaled in the market. However, if your product is not entirely innovative or somewhat revolutionary—not just *clear* Band-Aids—then a generic name is going to fall short of a consumer's expectations. Branding is no longer an add-on to a product or service in the marketplace. Consumers have become so savvy that they expect a product or service to be branded. There is no more perfect example of this than Chinese food. I have a friend who runs a Chinese restaurant in New York, where there are literally thousands of Chinese restaurants. For years, he operated as just another Chinese restaurant and had no real sense of differentiation. Then he simply renamed his eatery 'The Den' and added a few design touches . . . resulting in a noticeable increase in his business."
—ABRAM SAUER, *brand analyst for Brandchannel.com*

" 'Sting' is a great name for the rock-jazz performer. Say it, and it conjures up every piece of information you have about the artist. If you're a Sting fan, the very mention of his monosyllabic moniker creates interest and openness to new information and offerings. His name has become a defining characteristic and part of his entire package or story. Had Gordon Mathew Sumner's career been built around his real name, it probably wouldn't have been as 'sticky' and had the same positive effect.

"Generic names aren't, by definition, bad. They just aren't always good. The only reason Accenture is sticky is that they

have spent millions to promote it. Specific names are better—especially if they have emotional relevance and built-in distinctiveness."
—ALLAN GORMAN, *president of AGCD, a branding consultancy*

"Using a descriptive phrase as a brand name is almost always a bad idea, even though this is the best shortcut to communicating your product or service to consumers. A fanciful name or a completely made-up name is best of all because it can own a piece of brand and intellectual property real estate."
—SETH M. SIEGEL, *The Beanstalk Group*

Six Steps to Take Before Making a Decision

1. **Analyze how the market will receive the name.** For example, with supporting context, will the market get it? Will the name jibe with your strategic positioning of the brand?

2. **Assess or test whether there are any negative connotations or associations with the name.** Once you have boiled down the list of prospects, you can do some nonscientific polling (i.e., in shopping malls, bars, and at office gatherings). You can also conduct focus groups to test reactions further, or you can do a more expensive quantifiable study to gauge understanding, acceptance, likeability, or other associations with your prospective name.

   Is there a magic, foolproof method for testing names? No. In fact, sometimes too much analysis just delays decisions and defeats your purpose. I suggest you test a little, listen a little to people you respect, ask your gut, and make a choice.

   Naseem Javed, author of *Naming for Power* and founder of ABC Namebank, says, "Focus studies are a total waste. A small group of paid, doughnut-eating people certainly cannot gauge the success of a brand name." However, he does suggest testing a current brand name on the Web.[3]

3. **Do trademark searches to determine if the name is available for use.** (See Chapter 10 for more in-depth information on trademark searches and protection.)

4. **Look up your Web site address at Google.com, widely considered the Internet's most robust search engine.** If the name turns up more than a hundred other sites using your corporate name or portions of it, rest assured that consumers won't find your site unless it lands at the top of the results page.[4]

5. **Check your site's name on Domainsurfer.com.** Enter your domain name here, and all other registered domain names using all or portions of your name will pop up. The number of look-and-sound-alikes might surprise you. This is a reality check because, at the end of the day, your domain name must be a unique, one-of-a-kind title that is also easy to remember. Otherwise, you may as well write blank checks to your competitors.[5]
6. **Check your domain name on NetworkSolutions.com.** Look for the "ID Names" link. The site conducts a search in up to forty countries so you can see how many others are using your name overseas.[6]

If problems crop up (e.g., duplication, lack of clarity, an overwhelming number of look-alike businesses), your first priority is to reconsider the name you have chosen. Perhaps another name for your company or product is in order. Face it: No amount of fancy jargon or branding maneuvers will solve your problem, and no amount of advertising dollars will generate extra hits if your company or product has a bad or overly common name. So hang on to your marketing budget and change the name first.

Unfortunately, domain names are often the most neglected and misunderstood component of the corporate communications strategy. Too often, they are left to the discretion of a Webmaster or trademark clerk. To organize domain name structure properly, you need an internal mandate under a corporate communications strategy and the right budget, not just the mere $30 registration fee. Remember that hits occur when somebody simply remembers a name, keys it in, and gets right to the Web site.[7]

Five-Second Brand Bites—What's in a Name? Everything!

1. A brand name is the master art of the Brain Tattoo.
2. The brand name and how the brand is executed are equally vital for a successful and sustained brand life.
3. Whatever your budget, divide it by the projected years of use and value. This formula applies to investments in corporate identities and taglines.

4. Before you begin, *determine* your goal, *analyze* the competitive landscape, and *nail down* other business and marketing issues.
5. A brand is an expensive commodity; don't waste your money on a name that can't stick or won't last a lifetime.

End Notes

1. The compiled list of the costs of some famous brand names is derived from NameTrade, the professional naming service division of Cintara. Copyright © Nametrade.com. Used by permission.
2. The list of brand name derivations (different styles of names) is from NameTrade. Copyright (Nametrade.com. Used by permission.
3. Author interview with Naseem Javed, commenting on focus studies and on testing a current brand name on the Web.
4. Ibid.
5. Ibid.
6. Ibid.
7. Ibid.

chapter 7

Four Engines of Brand Development

Creating a brand starts with a deep inner perspective, an incisive snapshot of your brand's purpose, personality, point of difference, and promise. Closely held, private companies often look to the founders for inspiration, but as companies and brands grow and as management evolves and changes, challenges can set in that make knowing who you are difficult. Some companies create committees that treat tough decisions like a political campaign and try to please everyone, never getting to the heart of the question. Others skip the self-diagnosis, or can't make decisions, or live in denial. In any case, without these early decisions about identity and an authentic profile, growing or creating a brand is difficult at best. The following strategies and concepts are necessary to any branding process, whether you are rebranding or starting a new brand.

Engine 1: Know Who You Are

Brain Tattoos start when brand leaders know precisely what their brand is. It's their unique mental mark, the sum of all the brand's characteristics. A Brain Tattoo is something you land on your buyer, prospect, stakeholder, and/or employee that creates a strong, loyal, emotional connection.

Can you define your brand in ten words? If you polled half your staff today, would they have the same answer? What is the driving purpose in your brand? What do you promise to deliver? What are your strengths and weaknesses? What sets you apart from the pack? What makes you smile?

Set Your Goals

Where do you want this brand to be in five years, ten years? If you don't know where you are going, how will you know if you get there? Do you have accountable goals? Do you want to build a brand and sell it? Go public? Pass it on to a family member, donate it to a charitable cause, or just have fun with it? Be goal-driven, and the process becomes easier.

Ask your staff, ask yourself, and ask your executive team the same questions. Do you all sing the same song, or does someone sing in a completely different language from yours?

Once you've done the internal check, ask yourself, what do the world and your market think? Do their impressions jibe with your internal poll?

While taking time to think through and write down these answers may be a painful burden, this exercise is critical to building a brand strategy and mapping out a plan for market significance and success.

Define Your Voice and Your Vision

Branding is about lodging a collection of positive, relevant information in the minds of decision makers and influencers. Market share is good, but today mind share is equally as important. As consumers, we are assaulted every day with screaming brand messages. It's overwhelming, confusing, and often annoying. That's why it is so important for a company and its brands to speak in a singular, concise manner. Translate that to nonmarketing talk: Decide on what your brand represents. What are its most important characteristics? Next, describe your brand so that a child could understand it and repeat it!

Businesses with brilliant Brain Tattoos know clearly who they are. They are true to themselves; they are authentic and consistent in their behavior; they earn trust and a high degree of relevancy in the minds of their markets.

I'd been a loyal customer at The Container Store in Houston for years. I now live in Tampa, and there's no store here yet, nevertheless I remain loyal to the brand by patronizing the store on the Internet. With technology, brands have no boundaries, even when the geography is challenging.

The Container Store is always a fun, cool, shopping journey. Not only does the company deliver a huge and nifty assortment of organizational wares, the store experience makes you feel "a wow" of satisfying achievement. Maybe it's just me, a little on the anal side and slightly obsessed with tidiness, but I'm never confused or in doubt about "who" The Container Store is or "what" it is about.

Define Your Purpose

The Container Store brand is clear about its purpose. This company is devoted to helping people streamline and simplify their lives by offering an exceptional mix of storage and organization products. The Container Store is true to itself: It is a privately held corporation owned by two savvy entrepreneurs, Kip Tindell (CEO and president) and Garrett Boone (chairman). Their goal has never been growth for growth's sake. They adhere to a fundamental set of business values, centered around deliberate merchandising, superior customer service, and constant employee input. Growth and success have been the natural and inevitable result.

Tindell and Boone are heavily involved in all aspects of the company, and they can be found in the stores interacting with customers and employees. The passion for the company that employees feel comes from the top. The leadership and all the employees—the brand ambassadors—have a passion for their work and are creative, happy, friendly, and downright fun folks.

Define Your Personality

This brand is about innovative solutions to streamline your life. The Container Store's image is of a true connoisseur of every cool and hip container known. Those attributes resonate through everything—the company Web site, press kit, store interiors, displays, advertising, catalog, etc. Nothing misses a beat.

The same kind of thinking put into practice can work with any brand, in any industry. You just have to get a little creative, go a little deeper, and discover who you really are.

Engine 2: Be Unique

Just like a cattle brand, a commercial brand denotes a difference, a distinct mental mark that protects your asset so that no one can steal your thunder.

Many companies have honorable intentions. They even get excited when they speak of their brand spirit; nevertheless, they miss the boat and end up swimming in the sea of dreadful sameness.

Jack Trout, author of several great books including *Differentiate or Die,* says he sees two types of organizations. One type understands branding. They are out there doing battle with "higher quality" or good value or good old "better products." They feel that they are better than their competition and that the truth will win out. The other type of organization understands *the need* to be different, but, after some prodding, these organizations will admit that they just don't know how to do it. Their excuse: Our product or sales force just isn't that much different from our competitors' brand.[1]

According to Trout, "Choosing among multiple options is always based on differences, implicit or explicit. Psychologists point out that those vividly differentiated differences that are anchored to a product can enhance memory because they can be appreciated intellectually. In other words, if you are advertising a product, you ought to give them a reason to choose that product."[2]

Why not break away from the pedestrian pack, brand with distinction, and make a difference in your organization? Every brand in every category in every industry can be distinct. Brand leaders have to leave the zone of common thinking, make hard decisions, and execute and leverage their brand with reach, relevancy, and frequency to all points of contact with their market.

Many consumer product categories seem to grasp with comfort this "got to be different" notion, but many business-to-business (B2B) organizations completely overlook this opportunity to really power up their brand. Within the B2B landscape of so many bland brands, "being unique" is a huge competitive advantage.

Determine Your "Points of Distinction"

Of all the engines in brand development, being unique and defining your distinctive factors seems, by far, to be the toughest task. Figuring out your brand's point of distinction depends on a variety of factors, including your industry, marketing regulations, competitive environment, scale of your marketplace, social climate, business goals, and company and leadership core values.

A brand's uniqueness or points of distinction can derive from a variety of characteristics, attributes, and/or features. A brand can have one strong differentiator or a combination of two or more that create an inimitable identity. If you are serious about landing a mighty Brain Tattoo, you must brand big with a unique position, uncommon characteristics, or distinct attributes—otherwise you will drown fast.

How does your brand stand out? What is so darn different about you, your product, or company? To answer these questions you must first understand the meaning of the words *distinctive* and *unique*. I travel around the country and speak to high-level business leaders about their brand difference. Many with strong conviction contend that it's their "better service and higher-quality product" that sets them apart. Yet their competitors sing the same song, and both are lost among all the similar offerings and getting nowhere in the minds of their market.

In most cases, great service and quality product alone are not strong points of difference in a brand strategy. Even if they were truly accurate statements, most buyers are so jaded by this proposition that it's a very hard sell. Brand differentiating with the lowest price is also dangerous. Buyers hear this claim too often and are very skeptical—and, of course, competitors can easily drop prices and suddenly your "low-price spin" is just meaningless babble.

As a rule, I recommend companies in the brand-building process eliminate the generic, high-risk attributes of better service, better product, lower price, and bigger size (if your competitor starts buying up firms, suddenly you won't be the largest company anymore). Unless a brand can definitively articulate and own this space as a distinction, these perilous paths can be copied, beaten, or through mergers and acquisitions, become invalid. Some companies get it, and they have developed strong Brain Tattoos:

Differentiating Factor: A Brand-New Attitude in the Industry and a Memorable Icon. The employment services brand Monster.com (www.monster.com), for example, is full of an assertive personality, a "Why settle?" attitude, and a likable iconic character (a dashing purple monster) that is unlike any other player in their space. Before Monster.com came on the scene, this category had only a bunch of boring, look-alike bland brands.

Differentiating Factor: A New Combination of Hotel Market Positions, Business with High Style, and the Chicest "W" You've Ever Met. The W Hotel group (www.whotel.com) fused the business traveler niche with a high-style, hip image, creating a very distinct persona in the hospitality industry. This value-based, emotional bond is quite commanding with the changing demographic of a younger, cooler business consumer. The W says it all. W . . . for warm, wonderful, witty, wired. W for welcome. Whatever you want, whenever you want it—that's W.

Differentiating Factor: The Hip, Fashionable, and Always Embedded Target Logo. Target (www.target.com), a low-priced department store with a lot of the same merchandise and services as a K-mart store and Wal-Mart, is solidly positioned by its strong brand supported by brilliant, lifestyle-relevant advertising and well-merchandised stores with a consistently cool brand message: Expect more. Pay less.

Like a snowflake, a fingerprint—no two brands are identical. You must not be afraid. Put the work into it and uncover your unique factors. Successfully finding your point of difference is like adding 5,000 more horsepower to your engine.

By fully completing the "know who you" part of the branding process, you should have spotted some trends and identified one-of-a-kind characteristics or traits that can become distinguishing factors in your brand strategy. In a few industry sectors (i.e., legal, medical, government, and election politics), there may be marketing or advertising regulations that can affect your promotional strategies. Nevertheless, you can still adhere to these restrictions and use alternative, unrestricted touch points to communicate your difference to your market. In restricted markets, the key is creative execution of your difference. Possibly it's not a direct, in-your-face message—but a softer, more subdued, or subliminal approach.

As you explore points of distinction for your brand, ask yourself about:

➤ **Your Market.** What's relevant to the market's needs and desires?

➤ **The Competitive Landscape.** Are any of your competitors occupying this space (point of difference)?

➤ **Social and World Conditions.** Are there current events, attitudes, or recent wounds from an issue that would prohibit the market from opening its arms to your point of difference?

➤ **Copycat Protection.** Can someone easily copy or imitate your point of difference?

➤ **Longevity.** Will this point of difference be sustainable for a substantial period, get better with age, or quickly become irrelevant, out of style, out of mind?

➤ **Leverage.** Can the dog hunt? Does this point of difference have the legs to carry the brand? Can it be leveraged by many communication vehicles and tactics, or is it a hard difference to explain, demonstrate, or articulate?

Here is a partial list of possible brand differentiators. Not every one will apply to every product, company, service, or person. Sometimes combining distinctions with other characteristics can be a powerful strategy.

Sample Brand Differentiators

Credentials	Personality
Geography	Pioneer status
Heritage	Physical characteristics
Innovation	Social or environmental consciousness
Lack of something	Special ingredients
Mental attitude	Speed of action (fast or slow)
Niche markets	Style

I hope that your creative wheels are turning and that you have permanently freed yourself from the premise that your brand difference is customer service, better products, or your people. Those are fine things to have and can be blended into your big picture, but in most cases, they cannot stand alone in the battle of building a brand.

Think about some of the most memorable brands of our time. What distinct mental image comes to mind? Volvo: safety. UPS: the brown delivery uniforms, trucks, packaging. Southwest Airlines: low cost, no frills, and casual. The more unique the brand position (and attributes), the more protection you have from competition and the tighter your connection will be to your customers. This applies to any size and type of business.

Your brand should stand for something, be authentic and uniquely yours. It should be woven into every important decision and resonate through every point of contact with a company's market. Having a strong point of difference in your brand category is a major advantage in landing a Brain Tattoo.

Engine 3: Connect with Those Who Want What You Have

The brand belongs to the people. Without their minds being open to your imprint and your brand essence, you have nothing more than a company or product image program. As a brand leader you can guide and protect the result by:

➤ Authentically allowing your company to be itself and to know what its brand is

> ➤ Leveraging your brand's point of difference
> ➤ Expressing your brand's personality
> ➤ Delivering on your brand's promise

Even the most thought-out brand strategies and execution tactics have minimal value until they emotionally lock into a buyer's mind as a Brain Tattoo. It's human nature to bond with someone you like and relate to, and with whom you have a strong relationship. In most cases, these special friendships are earned over time and are based on a pattern of behavior and common values. Building a successful brand is a very similar process.

A true brand is honest and presents a demonstrable picture of the offering to the market. A prudent brander has determined that there are enough potential buyers (that can be reached) to provide a healthy return on an investment in a timely fashion. If there is no need, no desire, and no one willing to engage your proposition and pay for it, go back to the drawing board or consider your venture a not-for-profit hobby.

Understanding how your buyers and prospects tick and what motivates them will help make your message relevant, increase the odds of planting your brand in their minds, and create a lasting loyalty. Every buyer, in every market, both consumer and B2B, has a definable profile. It is built from needs, desires, values, and life experiences, along with behavior patterns established from gender, race, age, and geographical information. Regardless of what you are selling, these factors contribute to the buying decision process. Often companies fail to utilize this information in the mistaken belief that their buyer is unlike all other buyers. Humans will be humans. Their motivations may be different, but they are all cut from the same cloth.

Adapt to Change Yet Remain True to Brand

Once a brand structure is defined clearly, it must then find the buyers who want it. I'm often asked, "What happens when things like 9/11, a stock market crash, or other catastrophic event occurs and the market has very new needs? Do you completely reposition your brand?" Certainly, the specific situation is a consideration, but in general, I say *adapt* to the climate, but stay true to your brand essence. If you can't adapt without going far off your authentic mark, it's probably time to park the brand and create a new one.

The Jeep is a good example. When Jeep first entered the market, it was the off-road, rugged choice introducing four-wheel-drive engineering. Some sixty years later, the market continues to value the challenging, adventure-packed Jeep brand promise and persona. As the SUV market soars, a new demand for a more comfortable luxury product emerged. To contend with the shift, Jeep introduced new product options to meet those needs while remaining true to its core brand. The tagline says it all: "Legends evolve."

Market Opportunities Can Be Seductive. Business leaders, especially entrepreneurs, are often seduced by marginal market opportunities. You want to please everyone. However, losing focus on your core brand and market dilutes previous branding investments and is highly risky business. Don't try to please everyone. The result will be that you will mean nothing to anyone.

Focus Means Giving Something Else Up. Accept this, and move on. Single-mindedness and dedicated buyer targeting is much more efficient and powerful than a shotgun approach for landing a brand. If you build up a reservoir of killer ideas outside your brand, when the time is right, birth a new one.

Ask yourself, who is buying your brand now, and who do you need to add to that list? When I say buying, I don't mean laying out the cash and taking your brand home. I mean keeping your brand fresh in the buyer's mind. Remember that your market is composed of people who:

➤ Think you "are" what you represent.
➤ Are attracted to your point of difference.
➤ Admire your brand personality.
➤ Feel good about your brand promise.
➤ Consistently choose you over your competition when they need the authority in your category.

Most Brands Have Multiple Buyers. Their positive response to your brand will add value to your business model, and value converts to currency. The challenge with many brand leaders happens when they fail to adapt their brand message to meet the different needs of their buyer base. This does not mean you need to change your brand story or essence; it means you feed it to your buyers in their favorite flavor. Blanket communication smothers a brand and disconnects it from its audience. Be relevant, hit on emotion first, and then confirm with logic.

Profile and Target Potential Buyers. Some of the most common brand buyers are current customers, prospects, former customers, influencers, co-brand partners, vendors, your employees, your financial alliances and/or stakeholders, the community, government, your industry, and the media. Every business, no matter what its size, should profile its brand buyers and track their loyalty. If their loyalty is not solid, you have to work to solidify it.

Tracking loyalty can mean a number of activities, both in terms of size and frequency. Your profiling system can start as a simple spreadsheet with demographic, psychographic, and lifestyle fields, then evolve into a more sophisticated relational program. As a brand's volume grows (along with one's data files), there are multitudes of resources that can help map, clone, and enhance your buyer base.

Buyers of a Feather Flock Together. In every one of your profiles, you should see a driving sector of extreme supporters. These folks tend to be more loyal, have more frequency with your business, and spend or give the most back. These are your golden brand buyers. They not only need to be treated like royalty, but you need to watch their every move. What you learn from them will open the doors for a larger fan club, and fan clubs make referrals, and this is more gold.

The bottom-line goal is to get into your customers' heads, determine their motives, address their values and desires, and then trigger them to respond accordingly. Our world is complex, a melting pot of people with diverse profiles. The landscape continues to change. New generations, gender power, and ethnic and lifestyle groups are now driving our economies.

What Generation Is Your Primary Buyer Base? Are you speaking your buyers' language, recognizing who they are and triggering emotion?

Marc Gobé, author of *Emotional Branding*, believes there are three growing generational influences in most economies today: baby boomers, Gen-X, and Gen-Y. Each group has distinct attitudes and motivators, as follows:[3]

BABY BOOMERS	GEN-X	GEN-Y
(35-54)	(24-35)	(6-23)
Born 1946–64	Born 1965–76	Born 1977–94
81 Million people	46 Million people	75 Million people
Spend over $900 billion annually	Spend over $125 billion annually	Spend over $35–100 billion annually
Generation as Icon "Us"	Generation as Individual "I"	Generation as Philosophy "All"
Defining generation	Rebels/Influencers	Conscience
EXPERIENCED:	**EXPERIENCED:**	**EXPERIENCED:**
Rock and Roll	Disappointed children of divorce	Integration
Television	Driven to independence	Understand multilayered info.
Protests/riots	AIDS era maturity	Unity
Space exploration	Crack/gangs/violence	Optimistic
Vietnam War/hippies	Downsized parents	Reared in the era of psychology
Racial divide	Pop culture	Birth of the future
Sexual resolution	Information Explosion	Recycling
Yuppies	Today:	
New Definition of 50	Defy traditional structures	
	Entrepreneur	
	Highly educated/money driven	
	Taking charge to show power of	
	their voice	
RESPOND TO:	**RESPOND TO:**	**RESPOND TO:**
Cues of achievement/status/heroes	Themselves reflected in	New ideas
Iconic authority	images/messages	Companies with a philosophy
Trailblazers	Fierce sarcasm/imagination,	Multisensory experiences
Things that are earned	creativity	Multigenerational messages
Comfort	Stupid/smart messages	Messages that acknowledge they are
I've earned it luxury	Deconstructed paradigms	smart
Perks	Style	Fun/learning
Antiaging	Luxury goods and mass market	Parents as their heroes
		Interesting people
		Sense of community
EVOLUTION OF ATTITUDES	**EVOLUTION OF ATTITUDES**	**EVOLUTION OF ATTITUDES**
Icons–Rock and roll, movie, sports &	Alternative music/fashion	Breakthrough voices/talent with
political, business figures	idols/celebrities	messages
Marketing-influenced	Anti–marketing-influenced	Marketing-savvy
Race-divided	Multiethnic	Global culture
Realistic	Pessimistic	Optimistic
Technology-fearful	Technology-proficient	Technology-indoctrinated
Religion	Spirit/consciousness	Mysticism
Fortune and prosperity	Fame and fortune	Fun/interactivity
Escape/fantasy	Experience	Social responsibility
Aspiration	Inspiration	Fun nostalgia
Warm nostalgia	Hip nostalgia	Sexuality
Sex	Sexiness	Healthy attitude
Antiaging/longevity/mental health	Physical health/well being	Extreme sports
Male/female	Unisex	People

In addition to understanding how your buyer or prospect is wired, it's essential to keep in mind that things change daily, spanning significant behavioral trends that are also reshaping the consumer-buying environment.

Peter Francese, founder and now contributing writer for *American*

Demographics magazine, cites several evolving trends that will continue to have long-term impact on business and many brand categories. They include the growing power of women; an increasingly diverse marketplace; the entrepreneurial explosion; health care, aging, and alternative medicine; the rising demand for adult education; and the surging demand for luxury goods. Are there new opportunities here for your brand? Is your brand relevant to the widespread interest found in these movements?[4]

Astute brand leaders consistently connect with folks who want their brand, and they keep an eye on both demographic studies and future trend analysis. If you are to become an astute brand leader, you need to do the same. Three of the best resources for this information are *American Demographics* (www.demographics.com), the online newsletter *TrendSetters* (www.Trendsetters.com), and *Growth Strategies Newsletter* (310-451-2990).

Go where your market lives today and where your buyers will be tomorrow. Brand leaders who understand the entire spectrum of their buyers and not simply the narrow need they may fill with their brand will ultimately succeed. Branding is not about a simple transaction, but a relationship. Do you treat your market like a good friend you know well, or like a stranger on the street?

Brand Communication Is a Two-Way Dialogue. It's ongoing, and it's about speaking in your buyers' language and providing relevant information that improves their lives and connects to their deepest values.

Make Data Gathering a Priority

Every time you sell someone something that's good, or every time you sell something and add to a buyer's profile, that's an investment in your brand's future. Ask customers what's on their minds. Design a simple random or after-purchase questionnaire. Increase your response rate by rewarding customers who take action with a branded gift or something that symbolizes your brand promise.

Call Your Customers and Listen to Them. People love to talk—not necessarily to a telemarketing firm, but to someone from the executive team. Top management should not isolate itself from the buyer's direct voice. These "moments of truth" can be powerful. Create dialogue and listen a bunch. Don't just talk at your buyers. Engage them in a dialogue. In general, try to reduce the amount of static communication you have. This applies to advertising, promotion, Internet marketing, and doing business. These can be very casual channels or sophisticated research methods. A lot depends on your market and channels of contact. Invite feedback at many points of contact.

Gather Data Whenever and Wherever You Can. Without inconveniencing your buyer, always think about data gathering when structuring your brand contact points, promotions, events, or any communication. And don't forget the Web. This contact point is probably the easiest one to set up. If your brand has a Web site and you have no data-gathering point, shame on you. Money and new customers are sitting on the table somewhere.

Here are some ideas to consider (though not all apply to every business model), and remember to *always* gather profile information:

> ➤ **Invite customers to sound off**. Ask them what's bugging them (about anything) today. Make it fun, and reward the best gripe with a gift.
> ➤ **Get their opinions**. Conduct a survey about a new product or service.
> ➤ **Offer an e-zine**. Include stories, event announcements, tips, special offers, and humor. Make it meaningful, and remember: Don't overdo it—too much of a good thing is annoying.
> ➤ **Word of mouth.** Ask customers to tell a friend, add a link, or pass on an offer, then recognize those who do with a gift or service upgrade.

Create Customer Loyalty

When you connect to customers, you create loyalty. Some groups appear to be more loyal than others. As you might expect, the older people get, the more set in their ways they become. While this is true of everything from sex to pastimes, it is especially true for products and services. Women, for example, will experiment a great deal with both haircare products and hairstyles when they are younger, but, with each year, this desire for experimentation telescopes. In some cases, this is the result of exhaustion; in other cases, it happens because, after much searching and experimenting, women find what works best for them. My mother, for example, refuses to drive anything but a Ford, and my girlfriend—once happy to use my shampoo on occasion—will now go down five flights of stairs to the pharmacy to get the shampoo she needs. Sadly, this type of loyalty is not always earned. In some cases, it is just defaulted to by a consumer who no longer has the energy for continued experimentation.

All About Loyalty

"Niche consumers are much more brand loyal than the average. Take Apple Computer users. Apple users have a rebellious, individualistic, "bite me" attitude toward the rest of the computer world. This is possible because they feel they have the full support of Apple behind them. Apple has won this following by refusing to join the pack even when such refusals were detrimental to the company's bottom line. Perhaps as a result, Apple has become as much a lifestyle brand as it is a computer brand. However, I think such niche brand loyalty can only be won by example, not just advertising."
—ABRAM SAUER, *brand analyst with Brandchannel.com*

"Consumers over [age] 40 tend to be more loyal, and I believe that the great divide is that they came of age pre-Internet, at a time when great companies—many of which were custodians of great brands—engendered some reciprocal loyalty in their huge cohort of employees and service providers. Younger consumers are now—to borrow a phrase from the great sociologist Emile Durkheim—largely atomized. The brands that succeed best are those such as Amazon and eBay that allow consumers to 'have it their way.'"
—SETH M. SIEGEL, *chairman, The Beanstalk Group*

A brand is an emotional relationship between the buying market and a marketed product or service—a bond of loyalty, a connection of relevance and earned trust. The people own the brand. You direct it and protect it. The better you know your customers (inside and out), the more you will be able to connect with them and bond your brand with their brain.

Engine 4: Deliver a Great Experience

How does Starbucks get away with charging $3.50 for a cup of coffee when there is plenty of good coffee for a lot less all over town? Yes, their product is good, but a strong driver in their brand success is that they deliver a consistent experience that the market values and may pay extra for.

Starbucks is not a coffee shop. Starbucks is a destination where you hang out with friends and meet new ones, and where you feel like you belong to a community that adores the premium java bean and other hip refreshments. The staff is product-intelligent; the environment cool; the jazz calming; the merchandising is friendly; and no matter what state you are in, *The New York Times* is there to inform you.

Every business in every category has this same powerful opportunity to connect its brand to the market by the experience it conveys. Whether you have five employees or 50,000, whether you sell carpets or fish sticks, this engine is paramount to building your brand.

A brand experience is the journey, the adventure, and the trip you send your customers on when they decide to check you out or pay attention to something you are saying, when they determine to do business with you. The brand experience also extends after purchase—that is, after the customer has bought your product or service. Make it a memorable excursion.

The brand experience includes the tangible, the intangible, the big stuff, the little stuff, the things you say, the things customers hear, what they see and smell, and how and when you touch them. It is everything that bonds buyers with, or breaks them away from, your brand.

Points of Contact

So what does an incredible brand experience look, feel, or sound like? I had one such experience recently. It sounds like an oxymoron, a "feel good" dentist, but I found one. Flipping through a *Playbill* magazine during intermission at the opera, I noticed a small ad featuring two friendly-looking female dentists, both with glorious smiles. The headline read: A CARING AND GENTLE DENTIST OFFICE. I had been procrastinating for months about finding a new dentist and liked the idea that these dentists supported the arts, so I ripped out the ad.

When I called for an appointment, a pleasant receptionist answered the phone, and within thirty seconds I felt as if was talking to an old friend. She asked about my needs, my dental history, and when it would be convenient for me to come in. (How many times have you experienced a cranky, rushed, rude receptionist?)

The appointed day arrives. I'm dreading it as I do all dental appointments. My phone rings. It's the receptionist calling to make sure I know how to find the office and to say that they look forward to meeting me. I arrive at a small cottage-style building. A wooden sign in tranquil script names the practice and welcomes me. Parking is easy and feels safe. Inside, I immediately notice the flowing fountain. My stress lessens. The office is peaceful, beautifully decorated. Music softly plays, current magazines abound, and there's a refreshment cart. (Nothing like any dentist's office I've been to!) A cheery staff person greets me: "You must be Ms. Post. Welcome. So we can better serve you, would you mind filling out a few forms?" The forms show interest and compassion—not just "How will you pay us?" questions, but "How do you view your dental treatment? Are you an emergency, reactive patient, or do you like to be proactive?" I have not even met the doctor, and I am feeling less anxious.

Promptly after my forms are complete, I'm escorted to my doctor's private office. She carries in my chart and starts chatting and asking questions about me, my history, and my tolerance to pain. She listens and, after twenty minutes of getting to know each other, she walks me to the examining room. The examination was equally flawless. The experience was incredible; I almost forgot where I was.

A dental checkup is a relatively small purchase, although, over time, my worth to that business can add up. Numbers aside, for a small business, this one invested a substantial amount of time and resources to deliver a great experience. As a rule, as the ticket price for the product goes up, the quality of the experience should elevate too, but whatever the price, customers recognize and appreciate a quality experience.

Six Components of a Great Brand Experience

Whether you are building a brand experience for a company, product, or yourself, there are six major components you must keep in mind:

1. Mapping trails and touch points
2. Employing an aggressive customer loyalty strategy
3. Researching your customers' needs
4. Creating a three-part brand experience
5. Focusing on all the senses, to strengthen your customers' bond to the brand
6. Monitoring the customers' experience

Map the Trails and Touch Points. With every brand you manage or lead, a clear navigation path that keeps the relationship with the buyer and brand fluid is essential. By physically identifying these destinations and contact points, you can more easily enhance or adjust the experience. Every business or brand is a little different; however, these contact points can be adapted to most. If some of these touch points are not a part of your brand delivery experience, consider adding them to your mix.

A typical *business-to-consumer* (B2C) trail for a product sold through three selling channels—retail, online, mail order—might include these touch points:

➤ **Retail.** There are many points of contact with the customer in retail: parking lots, store entrances, the first people customers see, greeters, displays, signage, merchandise plans, self-service kiosks, TV monitors, product demonstration areas, customer assistance, packaging, rest rooms, fitting rooms, gift wrap areas, checkouts, return areas, customer service areas (remember, customer service also includes prerecorded phone messages, automated service systems, the hold message, and phone conversations), the pickup areas, drive-through windows, letters, thank-you notes, promotional flyers, advertisements, product warranties, and the actual product performance.

➤ **Online.** Examples are links through an affiliate or partner brand Web site, live customer service chat streams, e-mails, phone messages (prerecorded, automated service systems, the hold message, or phone conversations), letters, thank-you notes, promotional flyers, Web banners, advertisements, product warranties, and the actual product performance.

➤ **Mail Order.** Catalogs or flyers and the phone are the dominant touch points in the mail-order channel, though most of the same touch points used in online sales also usually apply.

A typical *business-to-business* (B2B) trail for a service sold through two selling channels—direct to business and online—might include these touch points:

➤ **Direct.** Phone (prerecorded messages, automated service systems, the hold message, phone conversations); in-person contact in the marketplace; all customer service; trade shows and events; networking; the provider's place of business and the prospect's or buyer's place of business; letters and thank-you notes; promotional flyers; contracts and service warranties; advertisements; and the actual service performance.

➤ **Online.** Links through an affiliate or partner brand Web site, live customer service chat streams, e-mails, phone contacts (prerecorded messages, automated service systems, the hold message, phone conversations, and all customer service), letters, thank-you notes, promotional flyers, Web banners, advertisements, service warranties, and the actual service performance.

Note that the phone point of contact appears each time, whether it is a B2C or B2B product, because the brand may have multiple call centers. What human layers are on these touch points (i.e., the brand ambassadors: employees, vendors, partners) and how do you touch them?

The market for each B2C or B2B touch point includes new buyers/ prospects, loyal buyers, and influencers. These buyers are looking for different things, and your brand message must meet all of them. For example:

➤ **New buyers/prospects** need a new, better, or different solution to a problem (whether their own or their business's or their bosses'); compelling emotion to draw them in; confirming logic to validate the offer; and extra reason or distinction for the buyer/prospect to select you over another choice.

➤ **Loyal buyers** require a consistent message to build stronger trust, compelling emotion to keep them from drifting, confirming logic to validate brand, extra reasons or distinctions to stay loyal, and recognition.

➤ **Influencers** are first movers, so trendsetter appeal is a requirement, followed by a consistent message to build trust, compelling emotion to make the influencer look good, confirming logic to validate the influencer's referral, and extra reasons or distinctions to keep this type of buyer interested.

Employ an Aggressive Customer Loyalty Strategy. This is a key element to building a positive brand experience that ultimately leads to a more meaningful and permanent Brain Tattoo. Once you mold your loyalty plan, then weave effective tactics into the experience you deliver to your customer. I asked loyalty expert and corporate adviser Jill Griffin, author of the groundbreaking *Customer Loyalty: How to Earn It, How to Keep It*, about the importance of this strategy in building a successful brand.

To Griffin, building customer loyalty means you have changed the customer's buying habits. According to Griffin, a loyal customer is one who makes regular repeat purchases, purchases across product and service lines, refers others, and demonstrates immunity to the pull of competition. Sure, these are tough standards and can vary a bit by industry, but truly loyal customers usually exhibit these four behaviors.

Attracting a new customer is generally much more expensive than taking good care of and keeping a loyal buyer. Therefore, a smart, well-planned brand experience that encompasses loyalty as a priority has extra legs—not only to please the customer, but also to deliver to the bottom line.

In establishing a loyalty strategy, you must first understand the distinction between customer service and building loyalty. Griffin explains, "When successfully building a brand, the customer's experience with that brand needs to be consistent with the image the brand projects. In other words, real experiences with the brand need to match expectations. Customer service is one important touch point in achieving that consistency, but to build customer loyalty, many other elements contribute to the customer experience besides just service. Marketing touch points, sales touch points, the way the product performs, the visual cues surrounding the product or service, word of mouth—all are contributors."[5]

Griffin, who is also the coauthor of the award-winning book *Customer Winback: How to Recapture Lost Customers and Keep Them Loyal*, advises companies to build their loyalty strategies around a customer's six stages of loyalty: suspect, prospect, first-time customer, repeat customer, client, and advocate. Says Griffin, "If your customer relationship processes and programs aren't moving customers forward, rethink them, and don't forget about focusing some resources on recovering lost customers." She adds, "Lost customers have surprising loyalty potential. Yet most companies treat lost customers as a lost cause."[6]

Carefully Research Your Customers' Needs. A brand builder regularly needs to conduct research to determine customer perceptions on the brand experience: "How are we doing?" "What do you value most?" "What can we do better to earn loyalty?" This process starts with qualitative focus studies to identify important performance attributes surrounding the brand experience. For example, customers using the Lands' End catalog would likely care about performance attributes such as on-hold time when calling the firm's toll-free line, service rep product knowledge, and so on. Once those attributes are identified, a brand builder then uses quantitative research to measure, compare, and rank them. Griffin suggests using quantitative methods to place the attributes into four actionable categories. Once you understand which of these attributes align with which category, your loyalty strategy comes to life!

However, Griffin cautions that customers' value definitions are constantly changing, so regular research is a must.[7]

> **Loyalty Drivers.** These are the attributes most important to your customers and where your performance is highest. Stay on course. Your efforts are already producing loyalty.
> **Improvement Candidates.** These attribute areas are important to your customers, but your performance is lacking. To improve loyalty, invest more resources to improve here.
> **Hidden Opportunities.** Your customers may have emerging needs that they themselves have yet to identify. Additional communication and investigation are warranted.
> **Overinvesting Candidates.** Since customer importance is low in this area, avoid overspending. Trimming costs may be wise.

As you evaluate your data, you should keep in mind there are some common myths concerning service, loyalty, and win-back. Create objective criteria when you are developing your game plan, and don't get caught up in these false perceptions:

Fallacy 1: Win-Back	A lost customer is a lost cause.
Fallacy 2: Loyalty	Once a customer buys from you, you've won his loyalty.
Fallacy 3: Loyalty	All customers are created equal.
Fallacy 4: Service	When they are unhappy, most customers will complain.

Staying close to customer needs through regular research is an important step in moving a repeat customer into a deeper loyalty zone, but there is more to do. Griffin recommends the following guidelines:[8]

Insulate your best customers from competitive attack. When you know a competitor is making a move on your loyal customers, take action. Touch your customers by giving them a gift, providing a special offer, or rewarding loyalty with a new level of value.

Make top spenders your biggest priority. Treat your top spenders like royalty. Not only do they generate the largest sales, in most cases they will buy across product and service lines and be your strongest sources of referrals. Keep them in top of mind and top of touch when delivering your experience.

Harness your supply chain to deliver better customer value and brand experience. Especially in the business-to-business sector, channel partners, affiliates, co-brand alliances, and collaboration are critical. This collaboration drives value and experience delivery.

Build a "frequent buyer program" that really works. The right frequency program can be a strong force in building loyalty. However, many programs with good intentions fail on execution and turn into a major brand experience deflator. Consider your customer's perception of valuable rewards, your resources, technology, and the overall ease of program execution from all parties involved.

Establish barriers to exits. By building in meaningful aspects to your brand experience and product or service performance, you can reduce the likelihood of customer defection. Retain valuable data and customer history to make future purchases easier, offer a unique service, and so on. These tactics make it harder for a customer to say good-bye.

Demonstrate "I know what you need." In the ideal brand experience, words like *appreciation, reorganization,* and *personalized* are powerful. With today's technology and especially the Internet, even small companies can blend these loyalty builders into their brand experience.

Hire, train, and motivate for loyalty. This critical part of the brand experience rests in the hands of the frontline employees. They must be hired, trained, and nurtured to support a culture of loyalty. In turn, employees need to be well treated, respected, and given opportunities to make decisions. By including your staff in the loyalty-building process and sharing the fruits of those efforts, you will empower a team that naturally takes special care of customers and adds value to your brand experience.

Design a program to win back lost customers and save those who might defect. A study conducted by Marketing Metrics found that firms have a much better chance of winning business from lost customers than from new prospects. According to the study, the average firm has a 60 percent to 70 percent probability of successfully selling again to active customers; a 20 percent to 40 percent probability of selling successfully to lost customers; and only a 5 percent to 20 percent probability of making a successful sale to prospects. Bottom line: Win-back can bring big rewards.[9]

Weigh the future buying potential of lost customers by tracking past purchases, looking at issues of dissatisfaction, and knowing their segment motivators. If you decide they are worth winning back, Griffin recommends that you ask, "What can we do to win back your business?" Then:

- ➤ Listen closely to what customers tell you.
- ➤ Meet the customer's requirements, and when you've corrected the problems that led to the defection, communicate the changes you made, then ask again for the customer's business.
- ➤ Be patient with the customer. Be open. Remember that some wounds heal slowly.
- ➤ Stay in touch with the lost customer.
- ➤ Make it easy for customers to come back to you. Avoid the "I told you so" stance.
- ➤ When your customers return, earn their business every day.

Win-back goes far beyond the bottom line. According to Griffin, win-back programs can help companies uncover improvement opportunities, help you pinpoint opportunities to improve product and service delivery, correct miscommunications, and identify new product opportunities. By analyzing lost customers, you can develop a profile for detecting at-risk customers and nip their defection in the bud.

A lost customer recovery program can help you limit negative word of mouth that may come from unhappy customers and encourage positive word of mouth from the customers who are regained. It stands to reason that if customers' concerns are left unaddressed, defecting customers can be a deadly source of informal negative publicity.[10]

Businesses that embrace loyalty as a priority in delivering their brand experience need to be aware of two significant changes in most buyers' behavior: 1) The Internet has changed the customer's perception of responsiveness, and 2) customers who engage with a firm through multiple channels exhibit deeper loyalty than single-channel customers do.

The only way a company can be successful is through loyal customers, which, of course, is a by-product of delivering a killer experience. What's more, it's just too expensive to turn nonbuyers into one-time customers and nothing else. The company (and brand) will die without more loyalty than that.

Create a three-part experience. The brand experience does not occur only at the time of a transaction. The brand experience begins as soon as you appear on the buyer's radar screen. By dividing the experience into three distinct time zones—before they buy, while they are buying, and after they buy—it's much easier to identify new opportunities and potentially dangerous challenges.

Focus on all the senses. A complete and winning experience should involve the buyers and take them to a higher place, an optimal state of brand bliss that's packed full of emotion, relevant connections, and imagination. Many brand leaders limit the experience to an obvious few levels. This is a big mistake, and shortchanges what you deliver to the buyer and the benefits your brand reaps.

Humans have five senses. These sensory points can all command an emotional response and strengthen the bond to the brand. What powerful opportunities are you missing to leverage your story and deliver a more pleasurable customer experience? Certainly, some businesses and brands may be naturally more conducive to high-sensory branding. However, all brands have opportunities to enhance their experience.

Ignite through the nose. Some people say that scent conjures more emotion than any other sense. Yet many brand leaders overlook this opportunity. Just a few places to consider adding scent to enhance your customer's experience may include in your:

Bookmarks	Packaging
Fabric or materials	Paper
Gift certificates	Press kits
Instruction manuals	Price or garment tags
Mailers	Product
Merchandise displays	Retail environments
Office	Thank-you notes
	Warranty package

Give them an earful. Sound effects can take a person just about anywhere. Imagine a calm rain forest that takes stress away or sizzling, snapping onions and fajitas (I'm getting hungry just writing those words). Sounds are influential. Music can energize, nature's voices soothe, laughter takes off an edge, and cheering adds momentum. What sounds would enhance your customers' experience and where would you place them? Think about using sounds in your:

Events	Press kits
Gift certificates	Product
Instruction manuals	Promotional CDs
Lobby	Rest rooms
Mailers	Retail environments
Merchandise displays	Telephone messages
Office	Thank-you notes
Packaging	Warranty package
	Web site

Focus on the eye factor. Our visual sense is very, very powerful. The nerve pathways from the eye to the brain are twenty-five times larger than the nerve pathways from the ear to the brain. The eye is the only sensory organ that contains brain cells. Memory improvement experts invariably emphasize techniques that link the information you want to remember to a visual image. The visual sense dominates all of the senses. In fact, Professor Albert Mehrabian of UCLA reports that humans gauge believability by three communication components: verbal (7 percent), vocal (38 percent), and visual (55 percent). Visual attributes outweighed everything in forming a credible impression. As you build your brand experience and develop communication to your market, don't underestimate the power of what your audience sees. Part of the brand experience is defined by your customers' response to colors, shapes, space, typefaces, photos, production quality, degree of complexity or simplicity, combinations of objects, and visual expressions through other art and images.[11]

Make sure your visual story is consistent and your image choices align with your message. Organize a visual audit of your:

Advertising	Press kits
Business forms	Product
Delivery vehicles	Promotional items
Environment (working and selling space)	Publications
Marketing materials	Signage
Merchandising	Training materials and manuals
Packaging	Uniforms
	Web site

Touch them so they can feel it. Whether it's a soft, comforting flannel fabric for a child's sleeping bag or an abrasive, scratchy cleaning sponge, texture adds a dimension of purpose, personality, and possibilities to a brand. As you execute your brand, try to incorporate different surfaces, weights, and touchable finishes. Touchy-feely characteristics can strengthen your message and add a new level to the experience. Think about adding touch to your:

Advertising	Press kits
Business forms	Product
Environment (working and selling space)	Promotional items
Marketing materials	Signage
Merchandising	Publications
Packaging	Training materials and manuals
	Uniforms

Savor the moment with flavor. Taste talks. By adding some flavor to your branding experience, you can open up a new world. Think about the meanings and associations of certain flavors and how they may add to your brand experience. For example:

Flavor	Association
Bubble gum	Playful
Cayenne	Aggressive
Chocolate	Sensual
Coffee	Energy
Curry	Exotic
Fruity	Fun
Mint	Cool
Vanilla	Calm
Wasabi	Intense

Now, consider how flavor can add to the potency of your:

Events	Product
Packaging (e.g., envelopes, stamps)	Promotional items
Press kits	Marketing materials
	Merchandising

As a frequent business traveler, I spend a lot of time in hotels. Recently, I had the pleasure of staying at Hotel Monaco in New Orleans. It is one of thirty-seven hotels owned by the Kimpton Group in San Francisco (http://kimptongroup.com). All are transformations of historic downtown buildings into charming, European-style accommodations where hospitality and service are paramount. In fact, their tagline is: Every hotel tells a story.

Founder Bill Kimpton built the company's brand on a philosophy that travelers "are all insecure. It's just a matter of degree. A hotel should relieve travelers of their insecurity and loneliness. It should make them feel warm and cozy." Today, this brand delivers that experience—indulging guests in a sensory journey—that exceeds expectations.

Hotel Monaco is both worldly and a world in itself in both attitude and décor, offering guests a mix of sophistication and urbane style. Upon entering the lobby, you are introduced to the brand's hip and whimsical personality—friendly staff, rich-colored, plush, comfy furnishings, and funky art. The hotel is vintage/eclectic and leverages every small detail to create a memorable time. Every sense is stimulated: *sight* (through the décor, furnishings, vibrant and rich colors, patterns, original artwork, hip staff); *sound* (a welcoming bellman, big band tunes filling the elevators, friendly conversation, wine-hour entertainment, in-room stereo and complimentary CD); *touch* (textures, fine fabrics, plush bedding, terry cloth robes and shower curtains, wine-hour massage, a hot shower or bubble bath, a helping hand, a welcoming handshake); *smell* (restaurants, room service, morning coffee service, Aveda bath products, fireplace, spas); *taste* (wine hour, decadent restaurant food, trendy snack selections, breakfast in bed, morning coffee service, and fresh-baked cookies at check-in).

Every point of contact at Hotel Monaco was a joy, including the bill. Kimpton properties are affordably priced. They know who they are—their brand is unique and breathes through their culture effortlessly, leaving the guest with a solid, defined Brain Tattoo and the desire to return soon.

Exceed buyers' expectations. The take-away and ramifications from any brand experience are by far the most chiseled memory in the mind of your buyer. The experience sets the tone for the relationship and the stage for future activities concerning the offering. A brand experience can range from a simple phone call concerning a product's performance to the long-term delivery of a complex service.

A positive experience can generate larger sales, repeat purchases, and new business. It can stimulate referrals, strengthen loyalty, and build trust. A bad or empty experience can create buyer tension, resulting in negative word of mouth and bad publicity. It can cause customer defection, damage your image, and strip the brand of its perceived value—and spawn more bad experiences.

A victorious brand leader must keep a current pulse on the expectations of the buyer through established monitoring methods, state and reinforce a brand promise, and deliver on that promise consistently. Your brand personality, purpose, and unique market position should direct the brand experience from the product you are offering to your employees, who are your brand champions; the media, who can be brand cheerleaders; and the stakeholders, who need confidence to keep the resources coming.

In today's competitive business world, there are many good companies vying for the same customers, singing the same song, and pitching the same products. Deliver a memorable experience that solidifies your brand, and customers will pay more for your offering and stick with you for a lifetime.

Monitor your customers' experience. Before you begin the brand experience process, it's always smart to commit to "wear your customer's shoes"—often. Walk through every point of contact as if you were a prospect, buyer, new employee, or even a vendor. Place an order, send out mystery clients, plant an applicant for a new position with HR, phone in a complaint, inquire as a media outlet, and e-mail a compliment.

The experience you *consistently* deliver is the backbone of your brand. Each touch point with it is like a vertebra, necessary for solid posture and brand strength. Examine your experience, look at all types of interactions, and work to enhance the experience every day. It's a wise investment in your brand.

Five-Second Brand Bites—Rev Up Your Brand

1. Before you brand, you must know who you are—what you are *made of*, what you *believe in*, and what you *stand for*.
2. A commercial brand denotes a difference; it is a *distinct mental mark*. Every brand in every category in every industry can be distinct; no two brands are identical.
3. A brand experience is the *journey* you send your customers on when they decide to check you out, pay attention to something you're saying, or do business with you. And it includes the *memory* of the experience after they buy.
4. A brand experience is the tangible, the intangible, the big stuff, and the little stuff.
5. Without minds open to your brand, you have nothing more than an image program. Brand strategies and tactics have little value until they lock into a buyer's mind.

End Notes

1. Jack Trout, *Differentiate or Die: Survival in Our Era of Killer Competition* (New York: John Wiley & Sons, Inc., 2000), p. vii. Used by permission of the author.
2. Ibid, p. 14. Used by permission of the author.
3. The generational chart is from Marc Gobé, *Emotional Branding*

(New York: Allworth Press, 2001). Used by permission of the author.

4. Peter Francese, "Consumers Today," *American Demographics* (April 2003), Primedia Business Magazines and Media, a PRIMEDIA company. Permission granted by publisher.

5. Jill Griffin, *Customer Loyalty: How to Earn It, How to Keep It* (San Francisco: Jossey-Bass 2002), pp. 31–32. Used by permission of the author.

6. Jill Griffin and Michael Lowenstein, *Customer Winback: How to Recapture Lost Customers and Keep Them Loyal* (San Francisco: Jossey-Bass, 2002). Used by permission of the authors.

7. Griffin and Lowenstein; and Griffin, p.138. Used by permission of the authors.

8. Griffin. Used by permission of the author.

9. Griffin. Used by permission of the author.

10. Griffin and Lowenstein. Used by permission of the author.

11. Bert Decker, *You've Got to Be Believed to Be Heard* (New York: St. Martin's Press, 1992), p. 81. Copyright © 1992 by Bert Decker. Reprinted by permission of St. Martin's Press, LLC.

The Fifth Engine: Eleven Tattoo Tactics That Speak Loudly Even When You Whisper

The strategy is set. You clearly know who you are, you've decided on your brand difference, you've found folks who want what you have, and you've mapped out the great experience you will deliver. Now you must employ the big brand bang and let your message resonate through every point of market contact.

The next step in building your brand is tactical. What specific weapons are you going to launch, at whom, and with what frequency? How will you be heard, noticed, and remembered in a crowded, chaotic playing field, possibly working with less money than your competitors? I refer to this engine as "speaking loudly even when you whisper," by which I mean making sure that even your smallest effort is on target, relevant, and working to build the brand.

Many organizations bust the brand big-time here. They lose focus; spend megabucks on meaningless mayhem; and forget the basics of clear, compelling, and consistent communications.

Tattoo Tactics

Branding or tattoo tactics are touch points and avenues to get your story out. They can include graphic identity, advertising, partnerships, media relations, community relations, promotions, customer service, sales, merchandising, online presence, and alternative and buzz activities.

Each one of these categories should have a "big picture" strategy and then be supported by actionable tasks.

Exaggerate, Accentuate, and Eliminate

When you are designing a communication program for your brand, you must not forget that your audience is assaulted with thousands of brand messages daily and many of these messages are fragmented, convoluted, and downright confusing. To make sure your audience "gets it," my simple rule is: Exaggerate; don't be shy. Accentuate; put the spotlight on the important stuff. And eliminate all the wasteful, meaningless junk that does not significantly speak to your brand.

Run all your communication activities through the brand filter. If they are in sync with your brand's purpose, personality, and promise and scream (your) big brand (difference), then they are keepers. If they don't, but they are nevertheless awesome promotional or communication tactics, then look at what you can change so they can work for your brand. If it's still too much of a stretch, then just forget about them. There are always other killer ways you can spread the good word about your brand.

Many people think successful brands are built purely on advertising. In the past, many great brands were certainly fueled by major advertising campaigns, but in today's market, brand builders face new challenges in reaching customers that stem from:

- ➤ **Out-of-Sight Costs.** The cost of advertising space and production is prohibitive for many brands.
- ➤ **Opt-Out Options.** Consumers can change the channel, flip the page, or put their names on "do not mail" lists.
- ➤ **Message Overload.** Every day new avenues to touch the customer's mind open. The other day I noticed the taxicab's hubcaps had ads on them.
- ➤ **Trust Is in the Trash Can.** With all the high-profile corporate scandals, consumers are more skeptical than ever. Credibility is at an all-time low.

To survive in this strenuous climate, a new mix of marketing/communications and attitude is critical.

No Risk, No Brand

There's a road named risk, and it's the most direct path to brand success. That's right. Incredible communication usually takes a least traveled path. It goes where its competitors are afraid to go. It stands out from the crowd. It creates a memorable, distinct mark on the mind of its market. Do your marketing and communications look and sound like ten of your closest competitors'? If so, how will the buyer know it's you?

The Three As: Reach, Relevance, Repetition

Reach. Are you hosting an event, distributing your collateral, and buying your ad space or time in the right target zone? How long will that impression last? What is every eyeball or ear costing you, and is there another way to touch them? Does the math work when you add in all the hidden production costs?

Relevance. A great communication tactic should look, sound, and feel like your brand persona and be a relevant value to the buying market. Tap into the whole brain of your buyers. Don't just shove your product features down their throat. Most consumers don't like the way that tastes. Hit them where they live. Upset people. Make them think. Challenge them. Remember, brands are primarily emotional and only confirmed with logic.

Repetition. Whatever you do, without frequency you are hosed. Let me repeat. Without frequency you are hosed. In most cases, the average person needs to be exposed to a message at least seven times before it makes a tiny dent in the brain. So, if you are buying a sixteenth-of-a-page, black-and-white ad in a daily journal and running it once, the sales or awareness generated from that single insertion might not be your home run for that quarter. You must repeat your message (in all tactics) over time for it really to sink in.

Strengthen the voice, face, and body of your brand. There is no single magic tactic to land a brand. Your industry, market size, timing, and resources are all factors. One thing is certain, people don't respond to boring. Full-throttle creative thinking is the key.

Tattoo Tactic 1: Visual Identity

The footprint of a brand—your corporate identity, graphic system, or visual voice—can take your brand many good places. It can also head you straight into a wall if it does not accurately project what the brand is and consistently stick to the story.

Your Logo

In most cases the graphic system starts with a presentation of the brand name. This logo sometimes involves a typeface or letter style. It may include an icon or visual element. From there, it generally creates a "look and feel" or a continuation of the brand persona and message through a visual pattern of communication. FedEx has a memorable graphic system. It's a simple, straightforward letter style that conveys order, strength, and action. Cingular Wireless uses a contemporary typeface and an icon, known as Jack, as a playful symbol of self-expression.

Will your logo take you where you need to go? When selecting or creating a main identity, you should ask yourself:

➤ Does it produce the same image in black and white as in color?
➤ Does it reproduce well through a fax or copier?
➤ Is it scalable?
➤ Will it work well in other media (e.g., print, broadcast, and digital)?
➤ Can it grow into brand extensions?
➤ How will it translate in a global market?
➤ Can you merchandise with it, or create merchandise and imprint or embroider it on?
➤ Does it support your brand story?

A logo is not a biography of your brand, but it is the indicator of your brand personality and essence. Don't kill your brand with a bad logo before it even walks. Type, color, illustrations, shapes, patterns, texture, and how these elements are combined project a great deal about your brand. Some are classics and can be relevant for a long period, but others get dated and look like a bad polyester leisure suit. Here are some simple rules.

Rules for Creating a Great Logo

➤ Just because your computer has typefaces doesn't mean they are the right fonts for your brand.
➤ Color has definite psychological attributes and associations. Use them wisely.

- Simple and clean is always best.
- Avoid overused symbols. They will pole-vault you straight to the sea of sameness.
- Unless you are a trendy business model, aim for timeless graphic appeal.
- Copycat logos are just as bad as copycat names.
- The value of a logo or identity is great. Invest in the development of it accordingly.

Don't be tempted by preprinted templates for business cards, letterhead, etc. It does not matter how small your company or brand is, this is an unoriginal way to brand yourself.

Graphic standard manuals can help govern your visual identity. Once the main logo or identity is established, the mission is to protect its integrity and build an all-points communication plan. After defining the plan and proper usage for the logo, colors, typefaces, and other related communication styles, it can be helpful to enact a graphics standards policy. This can be a stand-alone guide or part of a more comprehensive branding bible encompassing all aspects of the brand and its correct execution. A print manual is a good place to start; however, if your company has an employee/partner intranet or passcoded section of its Web site, this is an ideal place to house and access the information.

A graphic system will consistently build your brand. Inconsistency dilutes all your other efforts. Run through this checklist and make sure your logo and identity are consistently applied and are working for you, not against you, in your:

Ads	Proposals
Annual reports	Radio spots
Brochures	Sales presentations
Fax cover sheets	Signage
Letterhead	Thank-you cards
Mailing labels	Trade show booth
Merchandise	Training manuals
Packaging	Training tapes
Personnel applications	TV spots
Personnel manuals	Uniforms
Press kits	Web site
Promotional giveaways	

A weak or inconsistent graphic identity is a bad starting place for a brand's life. Invest the time and resources into this tactic. It is a powerful piece of your brand.

Tattoo Tactic 2: Advertising

Advertising can be used to generate leads, sell product, advocate beliefs, persuade, calm unrest, and build brands. Advertising is the act of paying to showcase a message, and more. Advertising gives the brand builder a high-speed lane to the market. On the other hand, it is not immune to falling trees, lightning, bad weather, careless drivers, or an occasional competitor with wings. Smart advertising can fertilize the brand soil and aid in the brand's growth. Bad advertising can stunt development and even end a life. If advertising is part of your brand growth mix, do it right or don't do it at all.

FROM THE BRAIN TRUST

Make an Impression

"Many a small thing has been made large by the right kind of advertising."
—MARK TWAIN

Advertising is one of the few controllable opportunities for brand messaging. You pick the audience, prepare the message, and decide on the frequency. A great ad grabs your attention, connects to the emotions of your target audience, delivers value, and is memorable, meaningful, concise, and always consistent with brand essence.

Advertising Dos and Don'ts

Do be honest.
Do create dialogue with your audience. One-way copy goes nowhere.
Do complement the established brand's look and feel.
Do have white space; it brings more attention to your message.
Do include contact information.
Do grow big ideas into a series of ads.
Do stick with creative that's working.
Do match ad production quality with the quality of your product or service.
Do create a distinct look.
Do breathe your brand and all its essence.

Don't just sing your praises; speak to your buyer's real benefits.

Don't overload the message.

Don't ditch good ads before their time.

Don't look just like your competitor.

Try adding something new and compelling to your next campaign. Any of the following ideas can be brand-supportive, fresh, and relevant. It all depends on how you put your message together and if you are consistent with it. For example:

➤ Buy an unusual size insertion.

➤ Buy a normal size, then create your ad inside a more unusual size or shape.

➤ Try soft ads, such as a community public service or an advertorial (which looks like an editorial).

➤ Spotlight a great client or employee.

➤ Split your ad buy throughout one publication so it becomes an evolving story.

➤ Split your broadcast buy into many mini spots.

➤ Quiz your readers or listeners with Q&A. Start with the answer, then reward them if they get the question.

➤ Tease your customers with suspense.

➤ Run the ad upside down.

➤ Incorporate a game into your advertising.

➤ Add humor.

➤ Include unexpected testimonials.

➤ Stir up controversy.

➤ Introduce a surprising perspective.

➤ Create a bumper sticker.

➤ Write your message in a new way (e.g., tattoo, ice sculpture, in the sand, carved in meat).

➤ Speak in a different language (e.g., as if to address another country, another generation, another species).

➤ Compensate buyers for reading or listening to your ads; test them on content.

➤ Reward buyers for referrals.

Make the Media Measure Up

Media options are like a field of wildflowers. There are many different varieties, and mixed in with the pretty ones are the weeds. Target your ad spending as much as possible. Mass marketing is now called *mess* marketing. It wastes too many resources on folks who would never buy your stuff. Take your message to where your market lives. Even if your product is business-related, connect with your buyers' lifestyle needs and their trigger values. Frequency is as important as your creative. All markets are on advertising and information overload, so if you want your message to stick, repeat, repeat, repeat. Here's how to pump up your next media buy:

➤ Try alternative media. (Advertising is popping up everywhere, even in rest rooms and on police cars.)
➤ See if remnant space is offered. (Many national pubs offer unsold space close to printing deadline at a reduced price.)
➤ Add a bounce-back offer. (Buy this, get this.)
➤ Create a sense of urgency. Reward the first 100 respondents.
➤ Co-brand with another company and split the cost.
➤ Sell product placements of other brands in your ad.
➤ Start your own print media; create a publication.
➤ Sponsor a broadcast buy; produce your own TV or radio show.
➤ Mount your own outdoor billboard; paint a building or a street.
➤ Check out nature's media: the sky painting, the grass cutting, floating messages on the water.

Media buying is expensive, so leverage your buy to another level of awareness and brand building. Here are some other ideas:

➤ If it's a notable, credible media outlet, reprint the ads for mailers or blow them up as posters.
➤ Collaborate on a joint media promotion with the media venue you are buying from.
➤ If you've got something newsworthy, ask for editorial coverage or at least the contact path.
➤ If you try an off-the-wall idea on your creative or media, pursue publicity to cover it.
➤ Get overruns of the magazine for client gifts.
➤ Negotiate a special event.
➤ Bargain for a package of opportunities.
➤ Cut a deal in which the media sponsors one of your pet non-profit projects.

Great advertising can springboard a brand into the market. Delivering on your brand promise keeps it out there.

Tattoo Tactic 3: Brand Partnerships

Sometimes two brands are better than one. Collaboration with other brands, vendors, and distribution channels not only adds firepower and reduces costs, but it ultimately can strengthen a brand.

Partnerships can be as simple as two brands co-hosting an event or as formal as an agreement involving new selling channels, co-op ad spending, joint research, and licensing contracts. When choosing any brand partner, you should adhere to an established set of guidelines that complement your brand and meet business goals.

Consider these questions:

➤ Can multiple opportunities and long-term merit develop from this partnership?
➤ Are your target audiences compatible?
➤ Does the company have a history of other successful partnerships?
➤ If the other company messes up on anything in the course of your relationship, how will it affect your brand?
➤ Can you do this activity without the other company and keep 100 percent of the gain?
➤ Does this relationship open up new segments of buyers? If so, does anything need to change in your current marketing?
➤ Is the other company committed to this relationship with money and people?
➤ Is this an exclusive partnership in your category?
➤ Is the upside gain greater than the expense of time and money needed?
➤ Are the terms of this agreement clearly stated in a legal document?
➤ Is there a "get out of the deal" clause?
➤ What are the points of synergy in this relationship (e.g., co-op ads, events, promotions, publicity, shared customer data, cross-marketing channels, shared content, point-of-purchase materials)?

Licensing: A New Level of Profit for Many Brands

James Mammarella, a frequent contributor to *Brandweek* and a licensing and brand development consultant with Lifestyle Marketing Group, LLC, in New York, says licensing can provide fantastic benefits to a brand, both in terms of exploiting new market segment opportunities and in profitability.

While not appropriate for all brands, a licensing strategy is essentially a suite of methods by which to multiply the brand equity through partnerships. In other words, licensing is a way to enter markets more quickly and more profitably than you could if you relied solely on your own resources.

Who Needs a Partner, or a Licensee? "Take Polo Ralph Lauren," Mammarella suggests. "After having achieved broad and deep success in the apparel market, the brand needed to grow, and home furnishings was a logical 'lifestyle' extension. However, no one at PRL had the expertise or connections to make this happen. The company could have taken years or spent a fortune to acquire or develop those assets. Instead, it rapidly, convincingly, and profitably entered the home furnishings segment via licensing. The result was a masterful program with such key licensees as the home textiles giant WestPoint Stevens, which pleased the retailers and not only met consumers' expectations, but exceeded and raised those expectations for the entire brand, including very favorable feedback into the core fashion apparel business."

Pitfalls of Partnerships and Licenses. Mammarella adds, "Many companies avoid licensing or co-branding partnerships because there are potential problems when it comes to protecting and advancing the brand. Case in point, again, is Polo Ralph Lauren. Licensing has worked extremely well for the company and its shareholders, but it is a partnership system that cannot alone prevent a titanic clash of egos. Just such a clash [was] playing out during 2003 and into 2004 between PRL and one of its leading licensees, the apparel-sourcing powerhouse Jones Apparel Group. More than $1 billion in wholesale fashion business is at stake, involving several of the PRL brands, and [it is] sending shock waves throughout the department store industry and its main manufacturing suppliers and brand marketing houses.

"So with this said," Mammarella warns, "if licensing is a viable strategy for your brand, it absolutely must be approached from a strategic point of view—with every safeguard that implies, including more than one planned exit strategy!"

Tattoo Tactic 4: Media Relations

Next to cash flow, positive publicity rules. For decades, paid advertising buys drove many a viscous brand. Today the pendulum has shifted. Out-of-sight ad space costs and declining credibility among consumers has moved many brand leaders to a stronger mix of paid and earned (publicity) media focus.

Twenty-four-hour news, free-flowing information, and breaking reports offer vast opportunities to get your brand message out with an added layer of authority and third-party endorsement. Despite the cynics, the media has immense influence on the market.

Organizations that don't take full advantage of this powerful vehicle will miss sales, stature, and a substantial brand bang.

The Truth About Publicity

All Publicity Is Not Good Publicity. Whoever started the rumor that even bad publicity is good for you is nuts. Bad coverage, inconsistent messages, or the mishandling of a situation or a reporter can be a grave ordeal. Media coverage is a serious aspect of your brand and should be handled with care. If you do mess up, have integrity and clean it up fast.

Size Does Not Matter. Any brand, big or small, can earn publicity. You just have to be aggressive, stay creative, and know the ground rules.

Proactivity and Publicity Are Synonymous. Three kinds of news coverage can help you build your brand:

1. **Hard News.** This kind of news is the result of something timely happening that has an effect on, or is of interest to, a group of people.
2. **Venue (Journalist)-Driven News.** The media outlet has a subject in mind and goes out and builds a story.
3. **PR–Pitched Coverage.** Somebody suggests an angle, either a PR professional or a media-savvy individual, and the media source agrees with its newsworthiness and covers the subject.

All three kinds of coverage require planning and should be actively pursued. All three can launch a brand faster than you can say "bank on it." The number of media outlets has grown by leaps and bounds over the past twenty years. Besides mainstream news reporting, just about every industry or interest group has its journals and outlets (if they don't, there's a new opportunity for you to create one).

In addition to direct publicity with the blessing of an editor or producer, you can gain attention and spread your brand message using several other methods as well:

- ➤ **Letters to the Editor.** Sometimes these submissions are edited; sometimes they are not. This is an opportunity for you to spout off about your brand or some related matter that includes your brand.
- ➤ **Guest Columns.** Many news sources allow guest columns or spots. Some will even compensate you for your content. These can be an opinion piece, a how-to article, or a story.
- ➤ **Advertorials.** If you can't score with any other avenues on an issue, or if you simply want to supplement your message, you can always buy space or time and set up the information so it looks like editorial (hence the name advertorial). Other than abiding by the outlet's content guidelines, you should be totally free to express yourself here.

Whether you work with a PR firm or decide to manage this activity in-house, the following general rules of working with the press and building brand apply.

Create a Publicity Plan

As with all plans, your publicity plan should include your goals and the strategies and tactics that will help you achieve those goals. It should address how the brand story will be woven into all communications. To implement your plan, it's essential to:

- ➤ Decide on the chain of call and command for interviews. If leadership can't speak well or doesn't look the part, get professional coaching or select an alternative spokesperson.
- ➤ Create and maintain an up-to-date crisis plan for handling disasters, accidents, or the occasional "foot in mouth" situations.
- ➤ Develop a compelling and informative press kit that screams the brand. Make it available in print, online, and in a video (B roll or digitally) for broadcast.

Grab Attention and Honor the Integrity of Your Brand

In addition to the publicity plan, here are other ideas and examples for working with the media.

Create a creative press kit. Reporters are human and have been known to respond to creative things. Press kits and releases were not born to be boring. Have some fun, but make sure you include brand fact sheets, leadership bios, and releases, and use consistent language about your brand. Package your material with your brand in mind. Think about your purpose, personality, point of difference, and promise.

Schedule and proactively pitch news angles and photo opportunities.
The more distinct your brand is, the more natural news angles you have to pursue. Many times a strong news hook can spin into multiple messages that can extend to a variety of different media interests. For example, a printer that builds its brand around promising "No-stress service" could leverage this concept into several publicity, brand-building opportunities. Imagine . . .

Brand Name: Serenity Printing
Tagline: "Relax. We're doing the printing."
Point of Difference: How Serenity Printing views the act of printing; a great print job makes you feel good; working with pros makes the experience a breeze, so you—the business owner—can relax.
Unique Selling Proposition: The Serenity plant is designed like a spa. There's a nontraditional lobby with a huge mural (created by a local art class), new age music plays, a faint scent of ginger mists the air. There's a juice bar, a window display box showcases recent print projects, furniture is arranged according to feng shui, massage vibrators relieve customer tension, and the staff is dressed in light-colored lab coats.
Other: A loyalty program rewards best customers and staff with pampering services; graphics are soft and peaceful. Communications—from the Web site to the corporate brochure—is kind, calm, and customer service–oriented. Workstations are brand-focused, with heavy greenery and windows, and the plant's rejuvenating lunchroom is stocked with fruit and healthy snacks.

Here are examples of just a few publicity opportunities—in print, broadcast, and online—that might be generated by such a company:

General Business Section: A stressful industry de-stresses.
Human Resource Media: Company lowers turnover by lowering stress.
Lifestyle Section: Life and work balance.
Employment Section: Ten ways to enjoy your job more.
Community: The company mural was created from a high school competition.

Food Section: Eat for energy—how office munchies are changing at local print shop.

Marketing: Printing company really pampers customers.

Interior Design: Print shop adds Zen to its business environment.

None of these unusual traits takes away from quality printing or good service. However, by being different, a company can earn priceless publicity and a premier space in the minds of its customers. Think about what you can change in your business model that's newsworthy, supports your core purpose, and provides a memorable device to secure more brand equity.

Take advantage of current events. Offer your point of view on a piece of current news. Often something significant occurs in a market, and reporters seek perspectives on the issue. Respond in a timely fashion or you may miss the chance to speak your piece. Let's say, for example, that the breaking news is that a major national company is fined for deceptive advertising. Your company is an ad agency. Here is an opportunity to talk about how you avoid this situation. If your organization is a consumer-protection advocate, this would be your opportunity to speak out on the buyer's rights. Not only will you add fuel to your brand by contributing an added perspective, but you are helping the news sources do their job, thereby building a stronger relationship with them.

Create a new spin to an already-hot story. If a news story is hot and getting lots of attention from the media, often reporters look for extensions to the story. Sadly, the kidnapping of a high-profile executive overseas occurs. Your company sells business insurance for top executives. This is an open door for a story on protecting leadership. If your company is a travel agency, the event can lead to a story about high-risk destinations for business travelers and ways to ensure safety while traveling. Jumping on a high-profile story often means front-page coverage and opportunities to spread more of your brand message.

Monitor your coverage and leverage what you can. Consider a clipping service. Google offers a free online service—www.googlenewsalerts.com. Or, for a monthly fee, there are monitoring firms that cover broadcast, print, and online news outlets. This is also a good way to keep an eye on your competition.

Keep a file of all your victories and a log of all your lessons learned from the things you may want to forget. If you are a small operation, this may be merely a folder with all your publicity scores. If you have the resources, it's nice to tout good coverage on your Web site, thereby adding even more credibility to your brand. And always, always, always:

- ➤ Be conscious of your brand (its purpose, distinction, personality, and promise).
- ➤ Know the difference between news and advertising. Condense news information to the simplest, most straightforward language.
- ➤ Be honest, but remember that nothing is "off the record."
- ➤ Disseminate to touch points within one media source (e.g., print, broadcast, and online).
- ➤ Respect and nurture your media relationships.

Additional Idea Generators (may vary depending on industry):

- ➤ Break a record and get into the *Guinness Book of World Records*.
- ➤ Conduct a study, survey, or test, then publicize the results.
- ➤ Tie into a holiday. (*Chase's Calendar of Events* is the best source for every celebrated day.)
- ➤ Stir up controversy; do the unexpected.
- ➤ Think photo opportunity—big, many, and visually unusual.
- ➤ Produce an interesting annual event, a contest, or an exhibit.
- ➤ Be first by starting a trend or introducing a fresh way to solve an old problem.
- ➤ Prove your story with science.
- ➤ Involve kids, pets, and senior citizens.
- ➤ Turn mistakes into news.
- ➤ Assemble an advisory panel to review something.
- ➤ Engage a high-profile spokesperson.
- ➤ Tie into a sports event, make a bet, or create a rivalry.
- ➤ Go back in time and tie into an important day in history.
- ➤ Borrow an angle from another industry.
- ➤ Enhance your product with a good cause.
- ➤ Rename, repackage, or relaunch your product.

Tattoo Tactic 5: Community Relations

Community relations encompasses any niche community where having a strong positive relationship is important and valuable to the brand

and the market you serve. For many organizations, this includes your category industry and nonprofit interests.

Industry Goodwill

Building your brand in your industry can be as important as building your brand in the minds of your customers. Think about how having support and admiration from your business peers can positively affect your success by providing access to more collaborative opportunities, allowing you to attract new talent to your organization, attract media attention, and even gain referrals for business. All of this happens when people understand who you are and what your brand is about.

Communicate your brand story: its purpose, point of difference, personality, and promise with all points of contact. Brand-building opportunities can include:

➤ Event sponsorship
➤ Involvement in industrywide matters, such as:
  ❑ Underwriting of industry studies
  ❑ Organizing a volunteer pool of your brand ambassadors
  ❑ Producing or contributing to an annual event that recognizes top industry talent
  ❑ Running public service ads on the industry's behalf
  ❑ Supporting industry publications

Nonprofit Initiatives and Cause Marketing

This softer side of marketing and good public relations can open many doors to market segments, garner good publicity, empower employees to volunteer, and reinforce the brand's good citizen identity. Always make sure the effort is consistent with your brand's value and that, when appropriate, your brand is visible. Brand-building opportunities within the nonprofit sector can include:

➤ Sponsoring events and underwriting programs
➤ Serving on boards
➤ Organizing a volunteer pool
➤ Producing or contributing to fund-raisers
➤ Running public service ads on the nonprofit's behalf
➤ Advertising in nonprofit publications
➤ Setting up customer purchase programs that benefit the non-profit

Tattoo Tactic 6: Sales Promotions/Events

Promotions are any activities that stimulate purchasing. Promotions can work well in both consumer markets and the business-to-business space if planned and executed correctly. A great sales promotion can launch new products, reintroduce new and improved ones, clean out an old line or inventory, synergize co-brands, cross-sell among product lines, arouse loyalty, and entice first-time sampling or trial purchases.

Start with a Brand-Friendly BIG IDEA

This concept or theme needs to connect with potential buyers. Can they relate? Do they have an affinity with the idea? Is the idea true to the brand and its story? Get creative. Your big idea can tie into a current event, a product performance issue, an anniversary or holiday, an entertainment or sports venue or event, or a lifestyle interest. Run the idea through the brand filter for purpose, distinction, personality, and promise.

Include opportunities for partners or co-brands. These can be complementary brands, the media, or even some nonprofit organization that will help fuel the buzz. This not only spreads the cost but also can increase your market reach.

Create multichannel data-gathering and customer touch points. This increases customer contact with the brand and the experience, and also establishes an infrastructure to gather data at multiple locations: Internet, business locations, call centers, displays, events, and so on.

Build a many-legged program. In addition to direct paid promotion such as advertising, a super-promotion is interactive and newsworthy, and it's a story with many angles that will increase the opportunities for publicity. It will generate word-of-mouth buzz and Internet chat and offer a host of event possibilities from the promotion kickoff to the winner's party.

Keep it simple. Since a big part of the brand is the experience, a sloppy, dysfunctional promotion can kill loyalty and permanently damage a brand. Keep the logistics simple, do a dry run of the process, and if you fail in public, clean up the mess quickly.

Promotional techniques can include an endless list of fun and innovative ideas. They are not limited to big consumer companies. Business-to-business firms can enlist this thinking at trade shows, in direct-response ad campaigns, in direct mail, and even on the Internet to drive visitors. See if any of these methods work with your brand-friendly big idea:

- ➤ Contests and raffles
- ➤ Loyalty programs
- ➤ Gifts and gift certificates and branded giveaways
- ➤ Scratch-off discounts or prizes
- ➤ Free rebates, trial periods, and bounce-back offers
- ➤ In-store demonstrations and videos, CDs, DVDs
- ➤ Mobile locations and kiosks
- ➤ Seminars and teleseminars
- ➤ Incentive buying programs and bonus rewards
- ➤ Complimentary services and samples
- ➤ Events, tours, and exhibits

Tattoo Tactic 7: Customer Service

Serving customers seems like a simple task, yet many savvy business leaders are blind to the huge service cracks in their business. A crack in service is extremely dangerous. One too many rude encounters, another insensitive act, or a downright bitter battle, and your customer will not only make you history, but his rage can spread like wildfire and burn up even the best brand.

Is Your Customer Service Poor, Satisfactory, or Memorable?

Jeffrey Gitomer, author of *Customer Satisfaction Is Worthless, Customer Loyalty Is Priceless*, says it's one of the three. He also reminds us that the customer is "the" source of everyone's paycheck. Since that is the case, why is it that so many companies treat customer service like a stepchild when it comes to building their company or their brands? Customer service is one of the most vital factors in building loyalty, the lifeblood of brand; great customer service is as important as the oxygen in a respirator. Without it, your brand is destined for a painful death.[1]

In the end, therefore, the real boss is the customer. How you react and handle customers' problems will determine whether you are promoted or fired. Customers fire companies for:

➤ Showing no genuine or personal interest
➤ Unresponsiveness or unavailability
➤ Unfriendly frontline employees or poor or rude collection practices
➤ Overpromising and overeagerness
➤ Poor professional image, packaging, or product quality

When a customer fires you, there goes your brand along with it. Every customer you lose or disappoint eats away at your brand. They tell the rest of the world, and before you know it, your great product is shunned.[2]

How does customer service slip and fail big-time? Gitomer says organizations trip up when they:

➤ Use off-the-shelf mission statements that lack real meaning.
➤ Have no written principles on great customer service.
➤ Are unfriendly or rude or fail to speak to the customer's needs.
➤ Tolerate upper management that don't "walk the talk."
➤ Blame others instead of fixing the problem.
➤ Focus on satisfaction, not loyalty.
➤ Have low or no training budgets and train once in a while instead of every day.
➤ Concentrate on competitive issues rather than competitive advantage.

If any of these descriptions hit home, start making customer service a brand priority today. First, and most important, allocate the funds and time to develop a program that works with your organization and makes your customers happy. Next, train all your employees daily. Training is done in many and diverse ways, and not all of it is formal. Then, reward valiant efforts. Money, of course, is a great reward, but not all rewards are monetary—recognition and appreciation are strong motivators. Create a great service culture; integrate service into everything you and your employees do. Last, pay attention and listen a lot. Learning never stops.[3]

Customer Service Hot Points

Recent surveys have shown customer meltdown is most prevalent at these contact points, which should be checked regularly.

Frontline Service. The face of your brand starts with your frontline employees: your call centers, cashiers, and receptionists (traditionally low-paid employees). All too frequently, management does not spend enough time or money here. Make this a priority!

Phone Systems. I am a big proponent of efficiency; however, the math does not work if you lose customers daily because of some stress-inducing, nerve-pinching telephone system nightmare. Make certain your phone system:

> ➤ Offers the option of speaking with a "real" person.
> ➤ Projects friendly, happy, and helpful vibes in any recorded message.
> ➤ Provides information on peak call times, so customers can better manage their time.
> ➤ Has different on-hold options. Try humor, helpful hints, or trivia, depending on your brand.
> ➤ Always shows appreciation.
> ➤ Is user-friendly. Your contact directory should have an easy-to-use menu, and you should also provide live-person contact numbers.

Web Site. Most Web sites offer customers some kind of contact information for feedback, questions, or order inquiries. This is a nice idea if executed correctly, but it can also be a hot point for customer defection and major frustration. *BusinessWeek* reported on data collected by the Customer Respect Group on how long it takes to get a reply from the Web sites of the 100 largest companies. The findings: One-third of companies surveyed don't respond; the rest respond in two days (58 percent of the companies), three days (6 percent), and four days (6 percent). Fifty-eight percent is an admirable number, 30 percent is not. Where does your site fall? Brand-building Web sites make contact information points easy to use, friendly, and responsive.[4]

Unkept Promises. Many consumer and business sector brands offer warranties, guarantees, and rebates. All of these tactics add strong glue to the buyer–brand relationship *if* the process has integrity and the promise is kept. If it's not, it can appear deliberately deceptive, smell like a scam, and destroy a loyal relationship.

If you decide to employ one of these offers in your brand proposition, make sure the backend fulfillment and transaction systems are ready and can fulfill your promise. If you can't deliver, don't offer. Be straightforward with your terms, limit your disclaimers, and when at a crossroads, think about the consequences.

Every time your brand interacts with a customer, you have a great opportunity to build a stronger brand. The stronger your brand is, the more of these opportunities you will have.

Care for all your customers as if they were your best friend or your hero. Respect their needs. Make them feel special, treat them with no less kindness or compassion than you would want, and the big brand bang will follow.

Tattoo Tactic 8: Sales

Selling with brand in hand shortens the distance to the finish line. Selling today is no cakewalk. New products, trillions of choices, and floods of options surround us. Pressure is high, competition is everywhere, and the economy is faltering. So what. Quit your whining. Add some brand to your sales arsenal, and the process gets easier and more effective.

The Sales Bible author, Jeffrey Gitomer, says, "Customers hate to be sold, but they love to buy." Stop pushing product and start attracting people who want what you have—your brand. Become a magnet instead of a desperate commodity. By now (if you've followed my advice), your brand should have a clear essence, a defined purpose, a distinct point of difference, personality, and promise.

Infuse these brand components into your sales training, your sales process, and your sales tools with creativity and passion. You will be amazed at this newfound power. Add the brand into your sales training by producing branded events that empower sales excellence, building manuals and online and video tools with brand buzz, and branding a certification that becomes a brand extension.

Integrate the Brand into the Sales Process

Create lead generators through offering branded rewards, hosting branded informational seminars, staying in the face of the prospect with branded messages, and exhibiting at trade shows with a strong brand presence (business to business or business to consumer). Follow up with branded gratitude.

Include the brand in your sales tools. Produce proposals consistent with the brand identity. If you pitch your services or products through a written proposal, don't miss the road to building a bigger brand by throwing together some brand-bland document. If your brand is innovative, sell in an innovative style. If your brand is full of tradition, sell like the legend that you are. There is no law that says all proposals need to be in a boring 8½-by-11-inch folder. Open your mind. Present your package in a compelling, memorable way.

Design PowerPoint or other audiovisuals with brand standards. Nothing makes me want to run out of a meeting, screaming, more than a bad PowerPoint presentation. Here is your big chance for the floor, your opportunity to prove you are not like the rest and to showcase your wares, and you pull out a tired, copy-intense, clip-art rag of a presentation. Jump in your computer case now before anyone sees it's you.

Whatever your brand is, PowerPoint presentations are meant to aid the presenter, not distract from them. They recap data and convey messages. They are not book reports or pages lifted from an encyclopedia. Most of all, they should represent the brand. For better and branded presentations, consider the following guidelines:

➤ Use no more than fifteen words on a page.
➤ Use large-format photos.
➤ Keep pages simple. Less is more.
➤ Politely weave your brand logo into the design.
➤ Use type and graphics that are consistent with your brand personality.

Print your logo on relevant promotional giveaways. Printed promotional items are a great way to stay in front of your buyer and create brand awareness. With today's extensive assortment of printable items, there is no reason to waste money on items that don't sing your brand story. When opting to brand a giveaway item, ask yourself:

➤ Is this the best vehicle for our brand?
➤ Do our competitors use the same one?
➤ Is there an interesting way to package the item?
➤ Can we turn it into a mailer?

Don't think cost/item; think income/new or retained client. Don't think fast and easy to order; think relevant to the brand story. Take, for example, a management consulting firm:

Brand Name: Johnston and Peak, Inc.

Brand Promise: Brings strategic clarity to fast-growth companies.

Brand Differentiator: Transparent Transitions (a proprietary process for mapping and managing growth)

Brand Personality: Progressive, creative, and cutting-edge

Tagline: The Clear Choice

So that all communication reinforces the brand message, promotional items for such a firm might include:

➤ High-volume giveaways such as contemporary clear pens, clear clipboards, and clear pocket calculators with stamped or screened logos

➤ Holiday gifts for clients, such as a crystal box with an engraved inspirational message, filled with candy wrapped in logo-marked cellophane, with the logo and tagline printed on the bottom of the box

➤ Business cards printed on clear acetate and proposals bound in clear coil with clear covers

Branding is not a quick fix for a sales problem. Sales and branding work hand in hand to achieve business goals. A brand without strong selling is "a brand going nowhere," and selling without a brand presence has less horsepower and will make your sales journey a lot tougher than if you had included a brand in the process.

Incorporate your brand essence in all your selling initiatives. This will further connect you to the buyer, establish trust, enable you to stand out in a crowded marketplace, and build equity in your brand.

Tattoo Tactic 9: The Environment and Merchandising

Visual seduction is not just for retailers. Merchandising and environmental branding needs more respect. Once thought of as merely decorative displays or point-of-purchase sale stimulators, today merchandising and the environment are a significant brand-building tactic. In addition to traditional retailers, health care providers, business-to-business products, restaurants, entertainment venues, office buildings, and professional services can take advantage of simple environmental and merchandising techniques to drive revenue and build brand. Opportunities are everywhere:

➤ Do you have a lobby, showroom, or office where customers visit?
➤ Do you exhibit at trade shows?
➤ Do you sell your product face-to-face with a presentation?
➤ Do you have a conference room where deals are made?
➤ Do you co-brand with another company at events?
➤ Do you donate merchandise to charity auctions?
➤ Do you retail something traditionally not merchandised?
➤ Do you retail?

Having lived the life of a floor-planning, display-building, visual merchandiser early in my career, I know firsthand the influence and seductive command of strategically positioned product, message, and medium. My days of schlepping mannequins and props for a range of retailers and arranging merchandise taught me some basic disciplines for moving product and building brand in an environment.

Environments Created with the Brand in Mind

All visual, auditory, sensory, and functional aspects should communicate your brand essence. Wherever people congregate, you have an opportunity to merchandise. People like to look at stuff; they are curious and hungry for information, and often need something to do to pass the time. Think about where the people flock in your business channels.

Tell stories consistent with your brand. Branding is not only about shoving the product down a customer's throat; it's about painting a picture with a message. This can be accomplished by props, lighting, signage, and product organization.

Keep it simple and fresh. Most great merchandising is like fine art, showcased with care, design, and relevance. Less is better, and simple speaks volumes. If your traffic repeats or returns, make sure to rotate the message and keep the displays fresh. Customers are motivated by change.

Beyond Fashion—"Traditionally Not Merchandised" Merchandise

Throughout history, the fashion industry has leveraged merchandising and environmental branding as a proven way to build brands. Yet many nonretail businesses miss this opportunity. Anything can be packaged and merchandised, adding personality, purpose, point of difference, and promise—thus communicating your brand and a new layer of value.

Michael Colonna, president of the Visual Merchandising Trade Association (www.vmta.org), contends that it's no surprise to see visual merchandising departments spring up in industries such as banking, gourmet foods, and computing. The stretch of Park Avenue in New York between the 40s and 50s features several banking retail storefronts such as Fidelity, Dreyfus, and E*TRADE. The interesting thing about them is the sophistication of the window design and interior displays. An industry traditionally known for cheap furniture and bad artwork is making room for high-quality graphics, sophisticated type design, and very effective visual displays.

Even supermarket chains are showing strong signs of a visual merchandising renaissance, says Juan Romero, president of API, a retail environmental and brand design firm that specializes in the food sector. As product differentiation alone is no longer a guarantee for success, the entire retail industry is realizing that it's imperative to adopt a visual merchandising point of view in order to be able to communicate with the consumer effectively.

Attention all retailers: A hammer in the right environment can be just as sexy as a pair of strappy women's sandals. Target has done an incredible job of merchandising every piece of America's world, from cleaning supplies to paper products. The retailer uses simple, bold, life-style–focused displays and consistently weaves its Target icon into the design and presentation vehicles. If you need inspiration, whether you are a retailer or not, check out Target.[5]

Nonretail Merchandising Ideas

Lobby or Office. Don't just use art; create shadowboxes in high-traffic areas to feature product or client testimonials, or to spotlight employees. Brochures or collateral materials can often be part of lobby or office displays.

Showrooms. Showrooms generally have large open spaces. Use them advantageously. Make sure the scale of your display relates to the size of the room. Even nonsexy industrial products can be displayed with punch if they are grouped with large-scale imagery, other props, or multiples of the same product.

Trade Shows. While trade shows are an excellent forum for prospecting, customer interaction, and brand building, they bring a set of challenging dynamics to the merchandising task. Your competitors may have much larger resources to spend on show design, which can make you look very, very small. This is a problem only if you adhere to the lazy, noncreative approach to exhibiting. Think very big and simple. Understand that your space of operation is not just your booth but the scale of the show.

Always think brand, then think about the two different types of visitors to a trade show: the intimidated one who hates being pounced on and needs self-serve information, and the extrovert who loves attention and interaction. Consider creating uniforms for your staff or using unusual materials, such as colored crates, to create a feeling of size. Think about projecting a distinct style with fabric draping. Blow up images or compelling words and suspend them from above, or create a live display using live people.

Face-to-Face Presentations. Sometimes an added degree of merchandising when visiting a prospect can be a persuasive edge in closing a deal. Depending on what you are selling, think about how you show the customer your brand and what you stand for.

Do you whip your product out of a smashed-up box and say, "Here. Look at this"? Or do you carry the product in a branded container and then showcase it nicely on a display block or riser of some kind? If your brand is high-tech and innovative, consider merchandising materials that project that persona, such as rubber; clear, colored Plexiglas; and geometric shapes.

The same idea works when speaking about a process or service you may offer. Do you pull out a bunch of loose, torn papers and yap on, pitching your wares? Or, if your brand is traditional and conservative, do you pull out a stately, leather-bound, organized portfolio branded with your company identity? An engineering firm that specializes in environmental-friendly assignments could easily present a series of 12-by-12-inch display cards of recent projects framed in outdoor, natural elements. The carrying case could be a khaki knapsack with an embroidered logo of the firm. A follow-up could include a note with a pack of branded seeds symbolizing how the partnership will grow great things while being considerate to the earth.

Both of these ideas are simple and can add a lot of polish to a pitch and highlight the brand with the right choices of presentation materials, delivery, and follow-up.

Conference Rooms. Use similar ideas to those applied to lobby displays if clients wait in your conference room. Why not give them some eye candy in the form of a brand message? If you have bookshelves, empty a row and cluster some elements to illustrate a case study or a sample of your work or product line. Consider using a fish tank with a branded billboard inside, a pedestal display touting a superstar team member in your firm, or a wall of fame featuring students your firm has mentored. Any of these tactics can subtly build a brand message.

Co-Branding at Events. Do you co-brand with other companies at marketing events, underwrite expenses, share the limelight, and then drop the ball on merchandising opportunities? Anytime you invest time and/ or money to co-brand at an event, make sure your brand is properly presented. Consider a display that is brand-supportive and giveaways that are interactive and two-way, and make certain you have a data-gathering channel to follow up with more brand messaging. A cross-promotion, a time-sensitive value add-on, or just a thank-you will serve your purpose.

Donated Merchandise at Charity Auctions. Many companies give away products or services at charity events. The intention is admirable, but are they leveraging the brand-building opportunity? Most event producers allow a space to place your certificate on the auction table. Take this a step further and build a display that builds your brand. You've already got eyes on your brand. Why not tell the viewers your story? Every ounce of market touch counts when building a brand.

The Future of Retail Merchandising

I asked veteran environment guru Christopher Gunter, president of The Retail Group, a San Francisco–based firm that helps retailers and manufacturers sell products by developing branded store environments and point-of-purchase displays, for his thoughts on retail trends and how they will impact environments and merchandising in the brand building process.

"Having worked with hundreds of retailers over the years, from mom-and-pop merchants to international merchants [Sears, Radio Shack] and manufacturers [Whirlpool], what drives sales is not so much the product but the *promise*. What does the brand promise to deliver? What does the store promise in the way of experience?

"By design, and by necessity, the retail landscape is in constant change. Over the last few years, however, we have observed some significant metamorphoses in American retailing.

"The grocery channel has seen significant challenges of late," Gunter says. "Supermarkets, habitually challenged by small margins, also face massive consolidation and reorganization and, now, competition from super-centers and warehouse clubs. Consumers are increasingly turning to nontraditional suppliers of food [Costco, Super Target] for their staples and niche markets [Trader Joe's, the local farmers' market] for specialty items and noncommodities.

"While pundits have for years dismissed Wal-Mart's growth as merely an opportunity for other retailers to improve themselves, the fact is that Wal-Mart has and will continue to dominate many industry segments, driving countless businesses to extinction.

"Department stores have struggled, opening more doors for specialty retailers in many channels. Looking ahead, some existing trends will accelerate: Malls and retail operations will increasingly require reinvention, and simply adding an entertainment component will not suffice. We envision that lifestyle centers will continue to prove their relevance as consumers elect to frequent retail environments that reflect and reinforce their own lifestyle choices, rather than environments that simply line up national chains in a homogenous mix.

"The buying power and influence of Hispanic Americans will require national retailers to develop markedly different formats that, perhaps for the first time in this country, address the specific needs of one consumer segment."

In whatever way you create the environment, or whatever you decide to merchandise, run through this simple checklist to make sure it's making the right impression, stimulating sales, and building your brand.

➤ Is the merchandising or environment design "on brand"? Does it match the brand's purpose, personality, point of difference, and promise?

➤ Can you capture the image in a digital format and add it to your Web site?

➤ Are there multiple areas of opportunity to extend the message frequency?

➤ Do the environmental elements or the display scale with the space they are in?

➤ Can you add any interactivity or sensory components to the space or the experience?

If your display lacks that polished, professional image, find a freelance display person from a big retailer or go to www.vmta.org and post your merchandising needs. Remember, a cheesy display can be worse than no display at all.

Tattoo Tactic 10: Online

Building a brand, one thousand clicks at a time: Online technology has catapulted the brand like no other tactic. The impact on all business sectors and models is immense. Small companies can be global. Virtual stores can operate without inventory. Time to market is condensed to a warp speed, and the customer has more options and choices than ever before. As with every new horizon, there lie vast opportunities and difficult challenges.

Sure, you can build loyal communities, disseminate tons of information, and offer new and convenient ways to meet buyers' needs, but you can also create frustrating buying experiences, burn through earned trust, and dilute your brand equity as fast as you can say "Google."

Create a Web Site

The Internet is an awesome place to do just about everything, including adding more power to your brand. Business leaders who fail to keep up with technology and tap into this monumental opportunity, without doubt, will be left behind. A brand builder needs to think of a Web presence as a physical destination or store. Before launching a Web site, ask yourself this series of questions:

1. What are the objectives of the site in order of priority?
   - To sell product?
   - To provide information? If so, to whom (the market, suppliers, media, employees, stakeholders)?
   - To gather or exchange information?
2. Will you house several brands under one roof? Unless you cross-sell, is there a reason they are housed together?
3. Do you have distinct buying market segments with different needs? If so, you may consider several different sites addressing their needs in an appropriate dialogue.
4. Do you sell wholesale and retail? If so, in most cases, I would create two sites. The language and needs are too distinct.
5. Do you do business with different countries? If so, consider custom language links with relevant graphics.
6. Is your brand-name domain available?
7. If you have many brands, are they also available as domain names?
8. Have you secured all similar domain names with the .com, .net, and .org endings? If not, do what you can to acquire these names.

Otherwise, your customers may become frustrated, or worse, they could go to the wrong destination and defect from you.

Many companies have multiple domain names. This can be helpful with target marketing efforts or as a means to track promotions and advertising. If you are an existing company and can't secure a domain in your name, you may have to get extra creative and aggressive with how you communicate your address to your market. However, if you are a start-up brand or company, I strongly recommend locking in the domain name with the exact name of the brand at the outset.

Once you have sorted through your goals and targets, you must think brand. Just like a big department store, you can have a dominant parent brand as a point of entry with the look and feel of the main brand and then separate doors or links to enter the other individual brands. The reverse is also true. You can have an entry point into each individual brand with a link back to the mother brand. The key is that each brand needs to be in an environment that supports what it does, what it is, how it is different, and what it promises. Otherwise, it's a point of dilution for the brand.

Here's a simple formula for building brand with and on the Internet:

➤ **Emotion first, logic follows.** First impressions with emotion are important. Your front page is like your big display window. It's your image. What impression do visitors get when they visit your site? This does not mean you need lots of bells and whistles and flash. It means, however, that you need to allow the essence of your brand to shine through. Remember, a brand is an emotional connection to a buyer. It is then confirmed with logic. Does your site have instant emotional appeal or does it look like a yellow page directory?

➤ **Exude your brand essence.** Infuse your brand DNA in every visual and content element of your site. Address each of these questions:
   ❏ Is your purpose clear?
   ❏ Does your personality pop off every page?
   ❏ Can the visitor grasp your point of difference?
   ❏ Does he get what you promise?

➤ **Different strokes. Different folks. Different site.** If you have distinct markets as buyers, don't lump, clump, and mix them all up in one horrific mess. Either host separate sites or have clear links to take visitors to the relevant zone within your site.

- **Make the experience fun.** A Web site journey is another brand experience, so make it easy and memorable. Try to provide a site map or search tool if you have a great deal of information. Keep things simple and user-friendly. Capture everything in a condensed fashion for quick-read scanners, and then provide further links for more detail for those who prefer more.

- **Don't present conflicting images.** The quality of your Web site transfers to the perception of your brand quality. Are they the same? Do you sell some pricey, top-of-the-line product, but your Web site looks like a fifth-grade project? With the abundance of excellent and inexpensive stock photography and graphic images, there is no reason to use shoddy visuals that drain your brand quality.

- **Make it a two-way street.** The Internet welcomes interaction. Take advantage of data-gathering points. Invite visitors to opt into communities or receive something of value from you. Survey and poll your market. Listen to their feedback and incorporate technology into how you conduct business and transactions.

- **Grow through co-branding.** Don't lose sight of who you are or what you stand for; but at the same time, keep your eyes open for co-branding opportunities, online and offline. Co-branding can expand your market reach and sometimes even add clout to a younger, less established brand. This can be achieved though affiliate relationships, sharing content, bundling products or services, banner ads, joint promotions, or simple links.

- **Let them take it and run.** I'm referring to printable information about your brand that is on your site. I've been to many nice-looking sites and then wanted to print something for my file or a meeting and the page would not print. Always include downloadable PDF files on your company or brand facts and overviews. This way your brand identity is intact and your professionalism and quality travel to the next set of eyes.

- **Contact e-mails are for contact.** If you provide your visitors with a form or e-mail address to contact you, always reply. Otherwise, why have it? If you choose to structure a form with questions, make sure to give the sender an option to submit something in addition to your questions.

Leverage Other Online Tools

In addition to your Web site, there are many other effective online tools to build your brand: e-zines, e-mails, blogs, chat rooms, banner ads, promotions, and surveys. If you decide to use any of these tools, the same fundamental guidelines apply, along with an added responsibility of protecting your customers' privacy. Always provide an opt-out avenue, giving your customer a choice to participate or not.

Tattoo Tactic 11: Alternative and Buzz Activities

Guerrilla or alternative marketing has no rules. The more you can get away with, the better. Such campaigns are nontraditional. They disrupt and surprise. They can be crazy, irreverent, or bizarre, and many times they are extremely potent and effective for a lot less money than the ordinary campaigns.

An alternative approach can activate both consumer and business brands. Carefully constructed activities can certainly build brand momentum. Sloppy, shortsighted stunts can be suicide. The key here is thorough planning, exploration, and a response program for the worst-case scenarios.

Sam Travis Ewen, president of Interference Inc., a New York guerrilla and alternative marketing firm, offers these alternative options for brand building:

Branded free shuttle buses	Product sampling
Branded hitchhikers	Publicity stunts
Costumed characters interacting with the public	Random acts of kindness
Feet on the street	Street stenciling
Flyer distribution and posting	Street theater
Poster boards on lampposts	Stickering

Why Buzz?

Small talk delivers big *cha-ching*. Word-of-mouth referral, recommendation, or just plain buzz is an influential force in launching products and nurturing brands. The methodology is not new. It's been circulating for decades in a nonofficial manner. People talk, and when they like or dislike something, they tell others. Then others tell others, and before you know it, a new product is born, launched, or given the royal stamp of approval by a group of influencers.

The Value of Small Talk

". . . [T]he channel with the greatest influence in America is neither the traditional media of TV, radio, or print advertising, nor the new medium of the World Wide Web, but the "human"—individual, person-to-person, word-of-mouth."
—ED KELLER and JON BERRY, *authors of* The Influentials

In the 1980s, liquor companies, fashion-related brands, and record labels organized the practice and released squads of buzz generators. "Troops of talk" were released, primarily at lifestyle events, to stir up chat on new products, sport designer garb, or order up the latest beverage in a trendy bar. Today, this sleuth strategy is building brands in all business sectors. It is now a professionally serviced component of a marketing mix and used by many giant Fortune 500 brand names.

Why use buzz to build your brand? How does it work? Are there different kinds of buzz for consumer versus business brands? And where do you get some?

I first asked buzz guru John Taylor, president of Say So Marketing, a word-of-mouth event marketing service headquartered in New York City. He explained, "Marketing messages are so pervasive that they are no longer persuasive. The challenge to cut though the clutter and maximize a budget is monumental. Consumers tune out when ads come on. Even when people do remember an ad, they often don't remember who it was for. Costs are beyond reach, and many times we end up paying to reach the wrong people."

Word of mouth is sticky. A handful of people can influence an entire country. People believe word of mouth, not only from friends but from strangers. Sixty-seven percent of U.S. consumer goods sales now are influenced by word of mouth, according to information published by McKinsey & Company in May 2001.

How does buzz work? I also quizzed BzzAgent boss man Dave Balter, who sets up a beehive of Bzz in Boston. "Our brand of Bzz is about honesty. Our network of volunteer brand evangelists shares their honest opinions with other consumers. There's no deception in what we do.

Bzz is the conversation you had today about the movie you saw yesterday. It's the recommendation you made to your friend about a restaurant or a good book. It's completely natural. We harness what brand evangelists do every day: Communicate with passion about products and services they love. We allow our clients to capture real word of mouth and study how it's moving through the marketplace, and what types of people are moving it."

His firm manages, trains, communicates with, and deploys BzzAgents—folks who have an opinion about a product and want to share it with others. When BzzAgents create Bzz, they report it back to the "Central Hive" in exchange for feedback, training, and potential rewards. However, BzzAgents aren't in it for the rewards. Only about 30 percent of them ever redeem a reward. Why do BzzAgents do what they do? The most common responses are "for fun," "because I Bzz anyway," and "to get more involved with products I love."

Taylor of Say So Marketing refers to his army of buzz makers as "players." They are the butcher, the baker, the candlestick maker— anyone who has contact with the public!

Are there different varieties of buzz? You bet. Most buzz programs, like any communications effort, start with identifying brand objectives and then add a mix of execution tactics. Buzz is talk, chitchat, gossip, hearsay, rumors, opinions, e-mailed points of view, broadcast ranting and raving, and, of course, the sometimes-authoritative printed or written word. Whatever it takes to generate this buzz is where the campaign begins.

Because the nature of buzz is either on the Q.T. or totally top secret, the following examples are purely hearsay. Believe what you will and, of course, if the product is still available, tell all your friends.

➤ **Fake Controversies.** National retailer Abercrombie & Fitch, which markets to the irreverent college crowd, has been known to stir up a story or two. They promote a line of clothing with questionable slogans, perceived by some as politically in bad taste, and then apologize for the misstep and welcome the curious and rebellious shoppers.

➤ **Pushing the Envelope.** Microsoft launched MSN with a swarm of butterflies. Costumed, human butterfly buzz generators plastered New York City with thousands of branded butterfly stickers. Not only was the visual impact powerful, the company was fined $500 for littering, but garnered media coverage worldwide.

➤ **An Alternative Mixed Bag.** A combination of overt and covert tactics created a sphere of influence among targeted consumers for Sony Ericsson. With help from Interference, Inc., a huge buzz was created for its T68i mobile communication device and accessories. The campaign consisted of seven different elements executed in seven major markets:

1. **Leaners.** Attractive undercover actors visited popular happy-hour bars and clubs, struck up conversations with patrons, and introduced the phone into the conversation.

2. **Fake Tourists.** Teams of couples visited popular tourist locations (that were also popular with locals) and had passersby take their picture with the new T68i.

3. **Phone Finds.** Fake T68i cell phones were dropped in high-traffic, high-profile locations. When found, these phones prompted people to visit a Web site to enter to win a real T68i.

4. **Roving Connectors.** Street teams distributed more than 500,000 collateral pieces announcing the new product and promoting the online sweepstakes.

5. **Interactive Club Nights.** Patrons were given an experience that combined visual eye candy mixed with interactive text messaging.

6. **Airport Shuttle.** A Sony Ericsson–wrapped luxury shuttle bus provided free rides and live product demonstrations to business travelers.

7. **Golf Caddies.** Wearing the brand logo, caddies took pictures of foursomes with the T68i as they were waiting to tee off and e-mailed the photos from the phones to the customers. The campaign beamed with buzz and reportedly generated an estimated 30 million press impressions.

➤ **Business-to-Business Buzz.** Does buzz work in B2B contacts? "Absolutely," says Taylor. "Especially when a company is trying to be the hottest booth at a trade show. One technique is to pay speakers to weave brand names into their speeches and carefully training them so they don't go beyond the mission and ruin the entire approach." Crowded convention rest rooms and valet parking areas are also great hot spots for buzz.

➤ **Online Buzz.** A couple of years ago, two disgruntled travelers produced a hilarious and true PowerPoint presentation called "Yours Is a Very Bad Hotel." It chronicled a really bad experience with a national hotel chain. What started out as a story shared with five close friends ended up circulating to an audience of millions as it traveled the Internet. This situation not only generated warehouses full of publicity and Web chat, it is now a classic buzz icon and case study at many business schools.

Want Brand Buzz?

It's certainly out there to be had. However, most buzz aficionados suggest engaging professionals for several good reasons:

➤ A professional has learned most of the hard lessons of buzzing.
➤ One bad buzz can severely damage a brand.
➤ Poorly managed buzz can backfire, big-time.
➤ Since a big chunk of your brand equity comes from trust, one slipup could be a deal breaker.
➤ Outside buzz makers are usually more natural than internal brand teams, which tend to be in a "pitch mode."

Buzz campaigns can cost anywhere from a few thousand dollars to millions. There is no set price or range. Everything depends on scale: the number of people engaged, the number of hours they are engaged, the nature of the operation, the nature of the operatives (from students to senior executives to celebrities), the number of cities, travel costs, expenses, permits, and so on. One great buzz idea can also generate millions of dollars in return on investment.

All eleven communication tactics are the legs on the brand. Whether you've got a budget the size of Texas or the size of Rhode Island, there are many powerful, creative ways to touch your market and land your brand in their minds. When in doubt, run the idea through the brand filter. Is the tactic telling your brand story—that is, is it being true to your purpose, personality, point of difference, and promise—or is it just confusing your market and diluting your equity?

Five-Second Brand Bites—Tattoo Tactics that Stick

1. Tattoo tactics are the *weapons* you use to communicate your brand.

2. Your corporate *identity, graphic system,* or *visual voice* can take your brand many good places. It can also head you straight into a wall if it does not accurately project what the brand is and consistently stick to the story.

3. Good advertising is the brand builder's high-speed lane to the market. Bad advertising stunts development and may even end a life. Do it right, or don't do it at all.

4. Sometimes two brands are better than one. Collaboration with other brands, vendors, and distribution channels not only adds firepower and reduces costs, but ultimately strengthens a brand.

5. Next to cash flow, *positive* publicity rules.

6. Brand visibility in your industry pays dividends. It is a reservoir of talented employees, influence, and opportunities.

7. Promotions work in both consumer markets and the business-to-business space if planned and executed correctly.

8. A crack in service is extremely dangerous.

9. Visual seduction is not just for retailers.

10. Build your brand one thousand clicks at a time. Online technology can catapult the brand like no other tactic.

11. Guerrilla or alternative marketing has *no* rules.

End Notes

1. Jeffrey Gitomer, *Customer Satisfaction Is Worthless, Customer Loyalty Is Priceless* (Atlanta, Ga.: Bard Press, 1998), p. 42. Used by permission of the author.

2. Ibid, p. 59. Used by permission of the author.

3. Ibid, pp. 61–62. Used by permission of the author.

4. "The Big Picture: Anybody Out There?" *BusinessWeek* (August 4, 2003), p. 14, 2003. The McGraw-Hill Companies. Used by permission of the publisher.

5. Visual Merchandising Trade Association (VMTA.org). Used by permission of the VMTA.

chapter 9

Internal Branding: Breathing the Brand into Your Organization

Leading companies and organizations contend that their culture and people are the drivers and the foundation for their success. Unless you operate vending machines with robots, most would agree.

Still, a brand or a branded product is an asset you want in your arsenal. It adds value, instills confidence, creates loyalty, and reduces a buyer's risk. The natural combination of the two forces—people and brand—can create a harmonic, bulletproof winner in any economy.

Breathing brand inside an organization creates two distinct dimensions of power:

1. **The Brand Ambassadors.** Their function is branding the brand from the inside out. Employees are a loud voice to all organizational brands. They are the cheerleaders, the big brother or sister who watches out for the brand and serves as the human frontline to the market.
2. **The Employer's Brand.** This is the competitive advantage in a tight talent market, the magnet that draws out superstar recruits, empowers loyalty from current staff, and adds to the overall corporate brand.

Both disciplines require commitment, resources, and innovation. Both are worthy initiatives. The Conference Board, an international, not-for-profit organization that studies business trends, makes forecasts, and disseminates management information, conducted an extensive report on internal branding. The report, entitled *Engaging Employees*

Through Your Brand, looked at experiences and practices of 137 leading companies. As we walk through the process of breathing brand into your organization, I will cite some notable findings from this study.[1]

How to Create an Internal Brand

The size of your company may dictate how you manage and carry out these efforts. Larger organizations sometimes shift internal branding responsibilities from marketing to the HR department. In any case, the actions taken need to transform thinking about branding from a pure marketing function to an organizational principle. In all situations, leadership needs to be an advocate of all branding initiatives and assume an active role model position.

Internal branding goals may include:

➤ **Strengthening Your Brand's Visual Identification.** By establishing branding communication standards internally, the brand will move to the marketplace in a more consistent, cohesive fashion.

➤ **Launching New Business Units.** As organizations grow, new business units need to launch from within. Without that internal buy-in, the external branding process can be tougher.

➤ **Serving as a Catalyst for Change.** Layoffs, management changes, mergers, and acquisitions all shake up employees. The brand can serve as a security blanket through the toughest situations.

➤ **Being the Center Point for Your Brand Essence or Corporate Strategy.** The big brand is the glue that holds all the pieces together; it keeps everyone on the same page and focused on the company's mission.

➤ **Connecting Employees to Each Other as a Brand Family.** As humans, we all have tribal instincts. We like to hang together with like souls. Internal branding efforts can unite a tight team even in tough market conditions.

➤ **Achieving "Employer of Choice" Status.** Employees and recruits tend to gravitate to brands they understand, ones with clear identities, whose values they share. Recruiting top candidates and retaining skilled talent are the results of solid internal branding. Strong brands can reduce staffing turnover. Studies have shown that employees are more likely to stay with an organization that has strong positive branding. It gives them something to hold on to for security and a connection to shared values.

➤ **Instilling Brand Values in Key Processes.** As employees grasp the brand essence, they are more likely to infuse the same attributes into their work product and processes.

➤ **Delivering Brand Promises Through Employees.** Employees are the customer contact team. As they engage the brand promise, they will naturally channel it to the customers through customer service and all touch points.

➤ **Adding Momentum to Selling Channels.** Strong brands ease the selling process. If your organization has any kind or size of sales team, the more they know about the brand and believe in the brand, the easier it is for them to do their job. Without consistent communication supporting the brand, selling will be like trying to move boulders uphill in the rain.

From these goals, you need to decide if you create two separate initiatives or breathe brand in one unified effort. Your decision will depend on how closely aligned the corporate brand is with the individual marketed brands and the nature of your employee needs. In a simple perfect world, they would be closely aligned, but as companies grow, sometimes their diversification makes this more difficult.

Whatever track you take, you must tactically touch your troops with the appropriate brands.

FROM THE BRAIN TRUST

Branding and Organizational Excellence

"Ultimately, employer or internal branding can be a stimulus to improvement of all the people-related processes that create organizational excellence."
—Engaging Employees Through Your Brand, *The Conference Board study*

Employees are natural ambassadors for any brand. It gives them a sense of "feel good" responsibility and the opportunity to see the fruits of their efforts. Most organizations already have lots of communication vehicles, policies, manuals, training events. Why not weave the brand(s) in and make them working tactics for a desired big Brain Tattoo?

Companies polled in The Conference Board study, who rated their branding programs as successful, had several things in common. They had:

> ➤ Identified employees as a key target.
> ➤ Received a new infusion of funding dedicated to the employee communication effort.
> ➤ Involved their advertising in setting strategy, as well as in execution.
> ➤ Identified "delivering the brand promise to customers" as a key goal.

Tactics for Implementing an Internal Brand

The 137 companies surveyed by The Conference Board ranked the following general activities in accordance to their effectiveness (1 being most effective, 12 least effective):

1. Internal printed materials
2. Intranet campaign
3. Recognition and reward campaigns
4. In-house meetings
5. Management training
6. Role modeling by CEO
7. Role modeling by heads of business
8. Outside print and broadcast media
9. Variable compensation
10. Informal peer programs
11. Road shows
12. Formal peer programs

Inside branding adds muscle to your meaning. With these activities in mind, take the generic concepts and add some fun and innovation to breathe big brand into your internal organization. Here are some examples:

Environment

Lobby	Decorate in brand style on a special day or every day.

Lunchrooms	Brand your cups, vending machines, and napkins; label your water.
Rest rooms	Supply brand posters, branded TP, brand jokes bound in a book.
Working space	Install giant brand characters, murals, neon signs.

Communication

Newsletters/ publications	Think about Brandzines, Brandbuzz, The Brand Street Journal. Create newspaper funnies with the brand. Feature brand leaders, brand warriors, and brands busted.
Correspondence forms	Include everything from fax cover sheets to memos pads.
Annual report to employees	Prominently showcase the brands.
Catalogs	Use novelty items as incentives and rewards: stickers, bumper stickers, shirts, Jockey shorts, hats, other garments; or print up washable tattoos.

HR Functions

Applications	Tell a bit of your brand story.
Training/orientation	Explain how the brand was born and where it's headed. Test employees on brand knowledge, and reward them, too!
Welcome packages	If possible, give brand products and service to employees.
Performance reviews	Sprinkle the brand in the kudos.
Anniversary notices	Make it a thank-you note from the brand.

Events (brand parties and celebrations are a blast)

Unveiling of new brand	Christen any changes in a brand.
Achievement of brand	Throw a birthday party for the brand milestones.
Community affairs	Invite your employees to ride on the brand float.
	Sponsor branded teams that support hometown and employee interests.

| Internal branded merchandise | Select items that tie into your brand story. |

Measuring Your Success

Internal branding and enhanced employee communications can certainly be an expense. How will you know when and if it's working? From my experience, there are several observational indicators. They range from reduced employee turnover and increased employee satisfaction to increased productivity and overall customer relations and loyalty. More quantifiable methods can include surveys and one-on-one interviews. In addition, consider these two measures of success:

➤ **Breathing brand should be holistic.** The brand should be applied throughout the company and throughout internal and external markets. It should be known and understood. All employees must know the brand message and how it applies to them.

➤ **Your brand should be known in the employment marketplace.** Candidates will be familiar with the brand and will be attracted to the company because of it. Think of these examples: McDonald's is known for "food, folks, and fun"; Southwest Airlines for "freedom"; and L.L. Bean for the "outdoor enthusiast."

In the competitive environment of business, dedicated employee communications and breathing the brand into one's organization are synonymous with category leaders and success. Most businesses already have the basic information structure in place. Adding strategic, conscious branding-building methods into the formula will just elevate your victory.

Five-Second Brand Bites—The Breath of Corporate Life

1. Breathing brand into your organization should be a natural manifestation of the two forces (employees and the brand) creating a *harmonic, bulletproof* winner in any economy.

2. Breathing brand offers two distinct dimensions of power: *Brand ambassadors*, who protect the brand, and the *employer's brand*

identity, which creates the competitive advantage in a tight talent market and is the magnet that attracts superstar recruits, engenders staff loyalty, and adds to the overall corporate brand. Both require commitment, resources, and innovation. Both are worthy initiatives.

3. A successful internal branding program must identify employees as a key target, have dedicated and sufficient funding for employee communications, involve advertising in setting strategy as well as execution, and identify "delivering the brand promise to customers" as a key goal.

4. Measures of the success of internal branding include *reduced* employee turnover, *increased* employee satisfaction, and *greater* productivity and overall customer satisfaction and loyalty.

5. In the competitive environment of business, *dedicated employee communications* and *breathing the brand* in one's organization are synonymous with category leaders and success.

End Note

1. David Dell, Nathan Ainspan, Thomas Bodenberg, Kathryn Troy, and Jack Hickey, *Engaging Employees Through Your Brand* (New York: The Conference Board, 2001). Permission granted by publisher.

chapter 10

Before You Brand, Protect Your Assets

You have the best idea since sliced whole wheat bread. You spent a ton of time and money on a fresh new logo and a catchy name, and you just launched a very aggressive media campaign. Seems like a good day until you open your mail. "Excuse us," says the cold, edgy lawyer representing Company X. "Cease using that name or we will have you burn through wads of cash and make your life extremely miserable." A common result that comes from not investigating or securing intellectual property rights.

You've got a brilliant idea. It has big brand potential. It has modest, current value now, but you know with confidence it can grow to be something huge. At first, it may be simply a concept. Later it will become a name and eventually a brand name that can articulate a corporate entity, a product, a process, an event, a collection, an ingredient, service, or whatever you choose to brand.

Frequently, these names symbolize and communicate a brand story. They can also differentiate and protect a brand from imitation and copycatting. Protecting the turf of your brand name and/or marketing "phrases that pay," and making sure they are available, is serious business.

Where do you begin, and what can you truly protect? Global commerce and the Internet have fueled many thriving brand empires. They have also complicated the process of procuring, communicating, and safeguarding brand names.

*Information in this chapter is from the author's interview with Patricia Eyres.

My good friend Patricia S. Eyres, a national expert on intellectual property and litigation avoidance, calls herself a "recovering litigator" who knows firsthand the value of paying attention to prevention. After spending eighteen years defending companies in the courtroom, she resolved to help business leaders recognize potential legal land mines before they exploded into lawsuits. I posed some frequently asked questions to Patti—questions I have heard during my years working with companies in all business sectors. Here are her answers.

What is the difference between a trademark and service mark?

A copyright is a legal device that provides the creator of a work the right to control how the work is used. Copyright law protects the creator of text, graphics, photographs, sound and audio recordings, and all components of a musical work. Copyright ownership exists from the moment the materials are fixed in tangible form. The creator can then perfect greater rights by registering with the U.S. Copyright Office. This includes an infringement action seeking a court order to halt piracy and [claim] monetary damages.

The federal Copyright Act of 1976 is the governing law. It grants authors a group of intangible, exclusive rights over their work. These rights include:

> Reproduction (the right to make copies of a protected work)
> Distribution (the right to sell or otherwise distribute the work publicly or privately)
> Derivative work (the right to prepare new work based on the protected work or to create adaptations of the original or derivative work)
> Display (the right to display work in public)
> Public performance (the right to perform, act, or recite the work before a public audience)

The Copyright Act protects creative expression, not ideas and facts encompassed in the expression. The owner secures a copyright from the moment the work is fixed in tangible form, regardless of whether the work is officially published or registered with the U.S. Copyright Office. Thus, even unpublished handout materials, instruments, and visual aids are subject to protection.

A trademark is a distinctive title, phrase, logo, graphic symbol, color, or word that is used to identify a business, service, or product. Through trademark protection, you can distinguish your product or service from others in the marketplace. Trademarks are extremely valuable in establishing a brand. Trademark law specifies that "distinctive" means sufficiently unique, that it serves as an exclusive identifier of the goods or service. Trademark protection goes well beyond business names to unique colors, shapes, taglines, character names, and individualized expressions. One of the most valuable methods of building a brand through trademark is to coin a word or phrase that the law recognizes as "fanciful." For example, Kleenex, Kodak, and speaker Allen Klein's "Jollytologist."

A service mark is legally indistinguishable from a trademark and operates to identify a specific brand of service. The first business to use a trademark or service mark in the marketplace owns it and can legally enforce all rights associated with the exclusive use of the mark. I have used these service marks for more than two decades in the marketplace for professional speakers, consultants, authors, and distributors of educational and informational products.

Since you can brand other things beyond a company or products—a process, service program, a publication, or event—are there different search and register methods for these other entities?

The registration for copyright protection for a process, publication, or marketing materials involves two steps. As the creator of the material, you own the rights as soon as you complete the work. You own them unless and until you sell or give them away. You can put at the bottom the copyright legend [©], the copyright [name], and the year. You can also say "all rights reserved." For those potential "thieves" who are a little dense, you can also write "all rights reserved, including the right to reproduce in written or electronic form without the express written permission of the copyright holder." This tells people who might want to steal it that you intend to enforce your rights.

The advantage to this approach is that it is cost-free and puts all potential users on notice of your intent to enforce your copyright. If someone then infringes upon your exclusive rights without your permission, you can enforce the copyright in court. If successful, you may obtain actual damages by proving the dollar amount you actually lost from sales you would have made without the infringement, or damages in the amount of profits the infringer received; you can obtain those damages even if you haven't registered your work.

This approach limits you, however, from the full range of judicial remedies. Only if you have registered the work prior to the infringement, or within three months of publication, can you receive what are called "statutory damages." Because it is often very difficult—and ungodly expensive—to prove actual damages or unjust profits, statutory damages are set by law. If the infringement is innocent, the damages are less [$500], but with willful infringements they are as much as $20,000 to $100,000 per infringement. A court would take into account willfulness and the financial status of the infringer.

For valuable products associated with your brand, you are best served by registering the work with the U.S. Copyright Office. Advantage: broader rights for damages if you have to sue. Also, a [registered copyright is a] tangible asset for your company on sale. [You can download information on how to register a work from http://lcweb.loc.gov/copyright.]

To brand an event, such as the Annual Cancer League Silent Auction, you would register the name—and any distinctive graphics, font, color, image, or other unique identifying symbol—used for the event. The first step is to search the public database of trademarks at www.uspto.gov. Once you determine that the name is available, you can register online, or download the application form and fax or mail it to the U.S. Patent and Trademark Office.

What about when a person adds a name to their name as a tag?

This is ideal for trademark or service mark protection. For example, in my own business I have trademarked several taglines, which I use interchangeably, depending upon the nature of the speaking or consulting engagement: Patricia S. Eyres, Helping Managers Lead Within Legal Limits, or Litigation Management & Training Services, Inc. [whose tagline is]: Our Business Is Keeping Your Business Out of Court.

When you are starting to evaluate names for a brand, where do you start to search?

A good place to start is with a search of the Internet for words and phrases associated with your product or service. This type of search produces a wide variety of names, taglines, and associated terms. Of course, if you have a very individualized product or service name, you should take immediate steps to search the government database at www.uspto.gov. When you are able to confirm that nobody else has registered a trademark for the name or term, you gain maximum protection by immediate registration, which establishes your first use as a registered term. You can then use the trademark symbol [™] until you receive official confirmation of the registration. You can then change to registered trademark [®].

For those readers who have coined a word, phrase, or other "fanciful" product name but not registered the trademark, don't despair. Similar to the copyright protection you receive from the time a creative expression is "fixed" in tangible form, you may secure trademark protection from the moment you use a term in the stream of commerce. If you can establish the date of your first use, through business cards, brochures, or on a Web site, you will have superior rights to anyone else using an unregistered mark whose first use in commerce was later than your own. An important caveat is that both uses must be unregistered. Registration with the United States Patent and Trademark Office [USPTO], even well after [someone else used] an unregistered mark in the marketplace, immediately gains superior rights that are enforceable in the federal courts.

If you plan on doing business in other countries, what do you do differently?

No, registration with the USPTO is sufficient.

Does doing business on the Internet imply that you are doing business internationally?

The word *imply* really has no legal significance, although consumers may believe that a business on the Internet is capable of serving an international market. The Internet is accessible globally, and the law hasn't really caught up completely with the rapid pace of technological advancement. One thorny issue in intellectual property law is the question of "jurisdiction," meaning where the parties to a dispute can litigate their claims. Recently, a court in Australia ruled that a U.S.–based publisher of allegedly infringing materials could be sued in Australia, because it marketed on the Internet, and the owner of the material was in Australia. Federal and state courts within the United States are also having to address this issue more often, as the location of an Internet sale is not completely settled in the case law.

Does registration of a name on the Internet mean anything other than you have a Web address?

This is a great question, as this is another area of much confusion in the business community and even in the law. Registration of a Web site immediately establishes the exclusive right to use that Web site address.

It does not secure a trademark or service mark in the address, even when it is a distinctive name. While the registration of the Web site address does establish "first use in commerce" that is enforceable against all later unregistered users of the name, if a competitor registers that name ["mark"], intentionally or inadvertently, the registration will effectively create exclusive rights to use the name as a trademark. The result could be confusion in the marketplace, claims by the registered trademark holder that the Web site owner is "diluting" the value of the trademark, and other legal and practical problems. Accordingly, the best practice for anyone who wants to secure all rights to their product or service and build a brand should register both the Web site address and the name as a trademark.

Does a trademarked name need to be an incorporated company?

No.

Can you trademark a tagline? If so, do the same rules apply for use in other countries?

Yes.

If a name is available for trademark, but not on the Internet, does this create a problem?

If the name is available for trademark, the first registrant of the name will own it as a trademark, and a prior unregistered business or individual who has [the name on] the Internet cannot legally challenge the registered owner of the mark. It does create practical business challenges, as we've already noted.

Once you register a brand name, how long does the trademark last?

The protection lasts indefinitely, as long as you continue to use the mark in commerce. A potential "horror" is the loss of your trademark protection due to lack of use or inattention. The rule for trademark protection is "use it or lose it." Your mark will be presumed abandoned if you don't use it in promoting yourself or your business for three consecutive years. Likewise, trademark applications may be abandoned "if an applicant fails to respond, or to respond completely, within six months after the date an action is mailed." The application will be deemed abandoned.

Do you always need to include the trademark and other symbols?

It is best practice to include the symbol [and the ® after official confirmation of the registration from the USPTO]. It informs the public that the ownership is established and that the owner intends to fully enforce those rights. In addition, the more successful you are in establishing your brand, the more legal risk you run that others will use your trademarked brand name in the stream of commerce. In effect, you've "made it" when your brand is a household name. This is especially valuable when the mark is a coined name, such as Kleenex or Xerox. Under the law, the owner of the mark must take appropriate steps to enforce the mark and prevent it from becoming part of the general vocabulary. For this reason, you will often see Kimberly-Clark's advertisements in writers' magazines specifying that Kleenex is their registered name and the generic word is "tissue." Xerox Corporation makes similar efforts with advertisements reinforcing that Xerox is a registered trademark, and the proper term for reproducing something is to make a "photocopy."

If you notice someone is using a brand name you have applied for a trademark on, what should you do?

Let's assume that by "applied" you have registered the name with the USPTO. You can take several important steps. The first and most straightforward is to notify the potential infringer in writing. While e-mail is certainly an appropriate vehicle, the better practice is to send a hard copy letter by registered or certified mail, with return receipt requested. If you use e-mail, keep a printed copy of the message, and make sure it includes the date of transmission. The letter can be professional and does not have to threaten litigation. Simply inform the user of your brand name that you have registered that name and have the right to use it exclusively in the marketplace. Request that they discontinue using your mark—the legal term would be "cease and desist"—and give a reasonably deadline for them to inform you that they have done so.

If you get no response, or a negative response, the next step is to consult legal counsel in your area about the appropriate steps to enforce your rights. Counsel will need to confirm the status and effectiveness of your registration—or your first use in commerce if registration is not applicable. To minimize costs, your legal adviser will probably recommend a second letter on the law firm's letterhead, and court action only as a last resort.

When do you recommend organizations hire a trademark attorney instead of handling the name procurement and registering themselves?

The initial search of the USPTO Web site database and registration is not difficult. The database search is user-friendly, the time involved is not extensive, and it keeps the costs down. However, for any individual or business whose objective is to build a brand that will sustain a long-term professional career or a product involving significant investment of capital and resources, it is advisable to engage a service to do a comprehensive search and then to assist with the registration. This does two things. It provides a high degree of confidence for investing your time, resources, and money, and possibly to secure venture capital to build a brand. Second, in the very unlikely event that the professional you choose makes a mistake in the search or registration process and a dispute later develops, your representative's E&O policy [errors and omissions, sometimes called malpractice insurance] may be a source for compensating you for losses and, more important, indemnifying you against liability to a prior owner of the copyright or trademark.

Can you register a name that is taken if you are in a different industry?

Yes, generally you can apply to register a trademark or service mark if you are in a wholly different industry or geographic area, and there is no potential for confusion in the marketplace. The USPTO attorneys and staff who review the applications will determine whether the mark you seek can be registered without confusion, and you will ultimately receive notification that your mark is officially registered. If the registration process cannot be completed because of the earlier registered mark, you may be provided an opportunity to modify or change the look or language of the mark to satisfy the USPTO's concerns, and you can then reapply.

Can you share any brand name, service mark, or trademark nightmares with the readers?

In today's marketing environment, strong brands are created and maintained by using the Internet. Yet, some of the most significant horror stories occur with infringement of trademarks on the World Wide Web. For example, the use of similar trademarks on different Web sites creates a likelihood of confusion for site visitors, which may make it difficult to maintain your rights to the trademark that embodies your brand. A trademark owner may seek a court injunction to prevent a Web site from using your trademarks, but first you must establish that your trademark or service mark is entitled to trademark protection. If the trademark is not a fanciful or distinctive word, but rather a generic word or image, which must be associated with your distinct brand as a secondary meaning, the very fact of potential confusion may make it difficult for a court to order an injunction. Labrador Software filed a lawsuit against an Internet search service [Lycos] that used a black Labrador retriever image on its product. The court denied the injunction, finding that Labrador Software's mark was only descriptive and not entitled to legal protection absent a showing of secondary meaning.

Another area of risk with trademarks in cyberspace is the potential for your brand to be negatively impacted if your mark is linked to poor-quality products or sites that tarnish your desired image. Bally Total Fitness sued the operator of a site started by a dissatisfied consumer [Ballysucks]. The federal court in California refused to entertain Bally's complaint and granted a summary judgment, finding "no reasonable person could think Bally's is affiliated with or endorses the anti-Bally's site."

Because of the breadth of the First Amendment—[which extends to] the protection of free expression on the Internet—the court found that trademark law did not protect Bally's in this situation. Alternatively, when an adult Web site used the names PapalVisit and PapalVisit1999.com, trying to capitalize on a highly public event, the Archdiocese of St. Louis successfully obtained an injunction prohibiting the link of the trademarks to the adult site. The court found the marks to be distinctive.

Similarly, in Toys "R" Us vs. Akkaoui, the defendant used the Barbie trademark on an adult Web site. The court ruled against the site, finding that the use of the trademark, combined with distinctive fonts and color schemes associated with the Barbie brand, tarnished the trademark.

The more successful you are in creating a quality brand, the greater the likelihood that opportunists may dilute or infringe your brand for their own gain. Oppedahl & Larson is an intellectual property law firm that gained a national reputation due to its domain name expertise. The firm conducted periodic searches for its name on the Internet, which is a critical step to protecting your brand. Following one search, the firm discovered that its name had been used eight times as metatags on the sites of several organizations, and was ultimately forced to bring suits to stop the practice. Although the defendants were not actual competitors of the law firm, the latter's good name and strong brand were clearly used to draw traffic to their sites. The court found they willfully intended to trade on that reputation, which in turn diluted the Oppedahl & Larson trademark, and ordered a permanent injunction.

Finally, professionals such as lawyers, consultants, and professional speakers who use their own name to establish their brand should consider including a tagline or other distinctive logo [font, color, or other visually unique dimension] wherever possible. One nationally known speaker developed, over a period of years, a strong and immediately recognized brand with her own name. She then discovered that a newer speaker was using the very same name due to a formal name change. While it became clear that the name change was not an attempt to intentionally create confusion in the marketplace, it did just that. Fortunately for both parties, the issue was resolved with little expense and an agreement to yet another change of name. The best way to protect your brand is threefold: One, develop distinctive words, phrases, and visual cues to make your trademark or service mark stand out. Two, take all appropriate procedural steps to protect your marks through registration with the USPTO and continued use. And three, be vigilant in maintaining the integrity of your mark, including regular searches of the Internet to identify where and how your trademark or other intellectual property associated with your brand is being used.

Five-Second Brand Bites—Protect Your Brand

1. Got a brilliant idea? Secure your rights *now*. Always investigate whether the name is available *before* you start profiting from the brand.
2. A copyright is a legal device that provides the creator of a work the *right to control* how the work is used.
3. The Copyright Act protects creative expression, not ideas and facts encompassed in the expression. Copyright law protects the creator of *text, graphics, photographs, sound,* and *video,* and it exists from the moment the materials are *fixed* in *tangible* form.
4. A trademark is a distinctive *title, phrase, logo, graphic, color,* or *word* that is used to identify a business, service, or product. A service mark is legally indistinguishable from a trademark and operates to identify a specific brand of service.
5. The best way to protect your brand is threefold:
   ➤ Develop distinctive words, phrases, and visual cues to make your trademark or service mark stand out.

➤ Take all appropriate procedural steps to protect your marks through registration with the USPTO and through continued use (i.e., use it or lose it).

➤ Be vigilant in maintaining the integrity of your mark. Do regular searches of the Internet to identify where and how your trademark, or other intellectual property associated with your brand, is being used.

Epilogue: Top-Ten Tattoo Taboos

You've put in the hard work, spent the resources, and earned the gray hair—and, just like that, the brand starts disappearing. Momentum is flat, sales are down, employees are leaving, and even your brand partners don't want to play anymore.

What went wrong? Did you get lazy or think spending on a new set of golf clubs and country club membership was a smarter investment than a branding event with your blood-giving employees? Shame on you! Now you know what the brand blues feel like. Yet, there is still hope if you take immediate action.

Through my years in the branding battlefield, I've come to recognize the warning signals of brutal brand betrayal. It generally starts with some simple seduction by the devil of sameness, leading slowly straight into the gutter of the meaningless and mundane. It's such heartbreak—especially after a brand was off to a good start, full of fresh ideas and determined execution. Then, before the company knew what had happened, "Poof!" The brand disappeared, or all that remained was a faded smudge. Customers no longer knew what the heck the brand stood for, and they didn't feel any reason to select it over a brand they knew and trusted.

Unless you enjoy writing obituaries for your brands, avoid the following ten taboos at all costs. They will dilute your distinction, smear your significance, and create questions about your qualifications. In other words, they can bust a beaming brand quicker than you can say "brand bankruptcy." I share them with you in the hope that knowing them will help you avoid them, thereby saving you money, customers, employees, embarrassment, and maybe your business. Next to each taboo, I have suggested methods to counteract the taboo. Though I've numbered them for easy identification, all are equally dangerous.

Taboo	Counteraction
1. You believe a brand is your logo.	You know that your brand is the sum of all you do—tangible and intangible.
2. You are convinced your brand difference is your product/service or people.	You know that buyers hear that from everyone and that *different* means distinct. Brands that tout those sea-of-sameness words will soon drown.
3. When times are tough, you eliminate branding expenses.	When things are tough, you amp up all your branding efforts.
4. You swear you don't have time to plan.	You know that it takes less time to plan than it does to fix things because you couldn't find the time to plan.
5. You bought your administrative assistant a computer, therefore he is a designer. Your head engineer once wrote a poem, so she is a copywriter.	You know that investing in talented communication people and outside professionals is money in the bank.
6. You make your branding decisions based on what huge committees or your accounting department thinks. You think branding is a marketing thing.	You do your homework, enlist a small group of respected experts for their opinions, and follow your gut on branding. You breathe brand into every part of your business and every touch point with your market.
7. You change your branding graphics and taglines as often as you change your underwear.	You know that consistency reinforces brands, and unless it's hindering your brand or no longer relevant, you stick with it.
8. You think conformity is safe. You are adamant that creativity won't work in your industry.	You live by the motto: "No risk. No brand." You know that humans don't respond to boring, and your buyers are human.
9. You think mass advertising alone will build your brand.	You address all points of market contact as equally important in your brand-building strategy.

10. You spend more time looking at the past to create your next big idea.

You focus on all the new possibilities to solve any business challenge.

As I close this book on how to imprint great Brain Tattoos on your customers' minds, I've asked my good friend, Michael Tchong, to comment on the future of branding. His thoughts are shared in the Afterword. A trend expert, Tchong is my "go to" guy when it comes to learning what's next in any business or lifestyle movement.

If you don't subscribe to his Trendsetters report, you are missing out. Many of the greatest brand leaders are able to spot a market need way before it's even on most radar screens.

Deciding to read this book was an act of courage and indicates a desire to improve your business. I have presented a fresh way of thinking and provided practical tools and a formula to land a brand. If you are truly committed to your business, you can brand with brilliance and tattoo the minds of your buyers with your distinct story. I look forward to seeing your brand in lights.

Afterword: Branding the Future

Michael Tchong

Michael Tchong is an international trend analyst and founder of
Trendscape (www.Trendsetters.com).

A famous marketing quiz goes something like this: "If you
were to divide Coca-Cola in two with one part receiving plants, equipment, bottles, trucks and all other physical assets, while the other got
the brand, logo, and image, which one would you want to own?"

Any modern-day marketer would immediately choose the latter.
And why not: According to Interbrand's latest survey, Coca-Cola's
brand is worth some $70 billion. That's not surprising considering
"Coca-Cola" is said to be the world's second most recognized term after
"OK."

While media advertising dates back to the 1600s, it wasn't until the
1860s that soap manufacturers began the branding trend in earnest.
Then it took another 120 years for the value of "branding" to sink in,
which led to the Coca-Cola phenomenon.

*While there are certainly lessons from history, savvy brand leaders will
look forward to find the next big brand.*

Karen's metaphor of the brain tattoo and the brand is on target. It
encompasses not only the imprinting of your message on the mind of
your market, but, also the current popularity of tattoos, which once only
adorned the "lesser element," and is now a common body brand, which
further expresses one's identity.

Brands are personal expression symbols by those who consume them.

Studies show brand loyalty is declining. According to the international advertising agency DDB, only 63 percent of the U.S. population today sticks to well-known brand names, down from 80 percent in 1975. The Internet and other information technologies will only make it easier for consumers to flit among brands. The seeds of that trend are already evident in the popularity of online shopping comparison engines, which serve to minimize the roles of retail brands.

To combat this ramped brand defection, brand leaders have to brand with a distinct story, communicate creatively, and connect to the inner emotional values of the markets they serve.

Branding has evolved. Tomorrow's brands will be a new breed. Study this book—and build your brand to survive the test of time.

Resources

It's one thing to have a great brand, one that you love, bringing you tons of joy and/or a bunch of cash—but it's another to have all that and a keen eye and ear on great resources and talented people who can help get big things done in a moment of true tension.

These Web sites and book resources totally rock. I have learned so much from them, and am pleased to share them with you. Check them out and tell your friends. It may take additional funds to purchase some of these resources, but go for it. That's why we have credit cards—to feed our brains and support the branding world economy.

Web Sites

Branded Retail Environments

API: ArchitecturePlus International (ArchitecturePlus.com). Juan Romero, Tom Henken, and their team of talented folks have designed and branded some of the most successful retail environments. They understand the importance of total experience and alignment to the brand. If your brand environment needs a face-lift or total redo, contact API.

Branding

Brandchannel (www.brandchannel.com). Brandchannel offers a wealth of branding information from a global perspective. While this site covers a great many mega-brands, the content is valuable and diverse enough to be of interest to any size company. The site offers a variety of tools and information including listings for conferences, courses, and careers, as well as links to other valuable industry resources. Brandchannel is not a one-way street; it provides the opportunity for an open exchange on the subject of brands and branding from practitioners around the world.

The Center for Brand Research (http://www.centerforbrandingresearch .org). Led by Dr. Neal Burns at the University of Texas at Austin, the Center for Brand Research integrates academic and practical knowledge of the branding paradigm through study of best practices, careful case study and real world analysis, and partnership across a wide range of leaders of brand research and practice. Its primary purpose is to provide research opportunities that deal with both the development of branding theory and the practice of branding. Visit their site for more information on events.

Cintara (www.cintara.com). The name *Cintara* is derived from "cincture," to surround, and "tara," an old English word for excitement; therefore, surrounding your brand with excitement. The company evolved from a naming firm and design firm that together formed a full-service branding agency. Cintara does great work and has some excellent articles posted on its site, which is also very well done.

d/g* worldwide (Desgrippes Gobé Group—www.dga.com). The site of one of the top-ten global brand identity firms in the world, with offices in Paris, Tokyo, Brussels, New York, Hong Kong, Lyon, and Seoul. Marc Gobé (author of *Emotional Branding*) and his team create award-winning design, architecture, interactive, and packaging solutions for brands internationally.

Neutron LLC (www.neutronllc.com). Marty Neumeier (author of *The Brand Gap*) and his San Francisco–based team specialize in brand collaboration—the "glue" that holds integrated marketing together. Check out their site for upcoming branding workshops.

Business

Jim Blasingame, The Small Business Advocate (www.smallbusiness advocate.com). Since 1997, Blasingame has been hosting the nationally syndicated weekday radio/Internet talk show "The Small Business Advocate." Visit his site for show times (in live, replay, and archived formats), a free newsletter, and loads of articles by his Brain Trust, a community of business experts on every subject you'll ever need for business.

The Conference Board (www.conference-board.org). The Conference Board creates and disseminates knowledge about management and the marketplace to help businesses strengthen their performance and better serve society. Its Web site is a wealth of information and timely business reports.

TEC (www.teconline.com). Since 1957, TEC (or The Executive Committee) has been increasing the effectiveness and enhancing the lives of chief executives. Throughout the world, TEC members meet monthly and work on their businesses with peer executive leadership and other business owners. Additionally, members have access to more than 8,000 fellow executives, one-on-one coaches, and world-class speakers. The TEC site offers information on membership and many "best practice" business articles.

Competitive Intelligence and Market Studies

UCLA Rosenfeld Library CI Primer (www.anderson.ucla.edu/ resources/library/libcoint.htm). If you really are a market warrior at heart, here's a great place that details a step-by-step "check out the competition" process. The UCLA Rosenfeld Library has a site devoted to competitive intelligence (CI) that lists the questions to ask and links to the places to find the answers. The questions fall into three categories: the corporate picture (when did the company begin? how did it develop?); the industry environment (how are the products made?); and the sociopolitical environment covering outside factors. Some of the online reference links require paid subscriptions to access the databases, but there are also listed references that you can find in a library

Creativity

Creativity Thinking (www.creativethinking.net/). Michael Michalko is a leading creativity expert and author who specializes in providing creative-thinking workshops and seminars and facilitating think tanks for clients around the world. His site has books, resources, and many articles on creativity.

Customer Loyalty and Win-Back

Jill Griffin, The Griffin Group (www.loyaltysolutions.com). No one knows loyalty like Jill Griffin. She's authored three best-selling books, speaks around the world, and consults with some of America's top companies. Her Web site offers some great insights and articles into loyalty (how to get it and keep it) with your customers, which is a key part of brand building.

Design and Identity Specialists

Ad Medic (www.AdMedic.com). If you're not a Fortune 500 company or don't have the budget of one, Andrew Stoller is a great resource for fabulous print and Web design. A super-nice guy with lots of talent, who delivers great work for a really fair price. Check out his site and see for yourself.

Iridium Group (www.ir77.com). Dwayne Flinchum and Dennis Ahlgrim lead one of New York City's most talented firms. They understand the full essence of branding and create extraordinary visual identity systems and corporate marketing/communications programs. Visit their Web site to see their work and sign up for a free, thought-provoking and content-rich newsletter.

Guerrilla, Alternative, and Buzz Marketing

BzzAgent (www.bzzagent.com). The folks at BzzAgent love word-of-mouth marketing. They are experts. They've studied how it works, how it moves, and how it disperses through communities. This site is all about buzz. Spread some bzz, become a BzzAgent, sign up and get rewarded. If you want to hire Bzz for your brand, they can help with that, too.

Guerrilla Marketing Coach (www.gmarketingcoach.com). Want to learn more about the art of guerrilla marketing? Mitch Meyerson is the man. A consultant, Meyerson writes books and coaches professionals on this powerful business strategy. Plus he's been on *The Oprah Winfrey*

Show! His site has reams of good information and resources, and his coaching certification program gets rave reviews.

Interference, Inc. (www.interferenceinc.com). Sam Ewen and his team of guerrilla-marketing gurus help brands communicate with their target consumers through guerrilla intercept, direct promotion, street team marketing, alternative Internet marketing, stunt and publicity events, and high-impact, creative, attention-generating execution. They work with large and small brands and are a fun company.

Say So Marketing (www.saysomarketing.com). John Taylor leads this influential team of word-of-mouth masters. With experience derived from national agencies in advertising, direct response, sales promotion, and corporate communications, servicing many Fortune 500 clients, the company designs campaigns for both consumer and business companies. The Q.T. nature of this "top-secret business" prohibits me from telling you too much about them, other than they are very good at what they do. Their Web site is almost naked, except for the phone number to call to discuss your covert marketing needs.

Humor

David Glickman (www.davidglickman.com). One of the funniest guys I know, corporate comedian David Glickman provides clean, clever, customized comedy entertainment for conventions, meetings, and corporate brand events. He also offers punch-up services to make your material funnier. If your brand personality has a humor streak, consider tapping into Glickman's talent to rock your audience.

Intellectual Property Law

Litigation Management & Training Services, Inc. (www.prevent litigation.com). Patricia S. Eyres, a "recovering litigator," knows firsthand the value of paying attention to prevention. After spending eighteen years defending companies in the courtroom, she helps business leaders recognize potential legal land mines before they explode into lawsuits. Her Web site includes many free informative articles on intellectual property and updates to current law, and details her training and speaking programs.

Thomson & Thomson Connotation Services (www.thomson-thomson.com/). Trademark and copyright research firm Thomson &

Thomson offers two unique brand research services. Connotation Check and Connotation Evaluation will help businesses researching trademarks and corporate and product names for international launches to identify possible negative connotations and associations with their name in foreign markets—before costly mistakes are made. What does your name mean in another language? What do members of that country "feel" about the word as a name? Thomson & Thomson will help you find out.

TrademarkBots (www.TrademarkBots.com). TrademarkBots is a service that searches and reports each week on trademark brand names that are published on the Internet in trademark and domain name databases, the visible Web, chat rooms, message boards, publications, newspapers, and Web feeds. The goal is to identify potential trademark problems at an early stage, while you can still address them economically. You can register online for a no-cost personal introduction to TrademarkBots technology and services, which includes a sample report. You will also find several complimentary white papers that shed light on both brand clarity and brand clutter.

Licensing

The Beanstalk Group (www.beanstalk.com). The Beanstalk Group is the world's leading brand licensing and promotional merchandise management company. Beanstalk helps its clients license their famous trademarks, copyrights, and images, and develops promotional merchandise solutions. Seth M. Siegel, chairman of the company's licensing division, contributes regularly to *Brandweek*. His articles can be viewed at www
.beanstalk.com/licensing/experts/brandweek.html.

Marketing

Larry Chase's Search Engine for Marketers (http://wdfm.com). This is one of the coolest marketing Web sites around. Started in April 1995, it was the first e-mail newsletter about marketing on the Web. It's grown from an important audience of one to an impressive audience of over 125,000. Sign up and start receiving weekly reviews of the best marketing Web sites out there.

MarketingProfs.com (www.MarketingProfs.com). Marketing knowhow from professionals and professors. This is one of the best sites focused on the how-tos of marketing, both online and offline. Sign up for its free weekly newsletters.

MarketingSherpa (www.marketingsherpa.com). The site of the award-winning publisher of case studies, metrics guides, and how-to knowledge for marketing, advertising, and PR professionals. More than 125,000 marketers read MarketingSherpa's newsletters every week.

Marketing Virtual Library (www.KnowThis.com). Another leading resource and reference site on the Internet for those involved in marketing, market research, advertising, selling, promotion, and other marketing-related areas. Its chief goal is to offer a Web site that is committed to providing unbiased, objective information that will provide valuable tools for academics, business professionals, and students of marketing and related fields.

Naming/Language

NameTrade (www.nametrade.com). NameTrade is the professional naming service division of Cintara (see its listing under Branding). It delivers legally available corporate, product, and service names and naming architectures. The Web site has lots of cool naming insight.

Plumb Design Visual Thesaurus (www.visualthesaurus.com/classic). The Plumb Design Visual Thesaurus is an exploration of sense relationships within the English language. By clicking on words, you follow a thread of meaning, creating a spatial map of linguistic associations. The Visual Thesaurus was built using Thinkmap, a data-animation technology developed by Plumb Design.

Wordlab (www.wordlab.com). One of my favorite sites, it has everything you want to know about words, and most of it is free. Cool tools, links, and bizarre stuff, Wordlab is a unique mix of entertainment, enlightenment, encouragement, entropy, and e-formation. At Wordlab, they start at the far-out and keep on going.

PowerPoint Presentations

Social Media (www.sociablemedia.com). Effective communication is critical to landing your brand, yet so many professionals use terrible PowerPoint presentations. If you need help, check out my friend Cliff Atkinson. His work will blow you away. His prices are worthy of your time and brand. He does cleanup work and total redos, and he offers courses for your staff.

Sales

Jeffrey Gitomer (www.gitomer.com). Meet the godfather of selling, Jeffrey Gitomer. This guy could empower and inspire a rock to sell. Gitomer writes a weekly column, conducts workshops all over the world, cranks out great books, produces a weekly e-zine called Sales Caffeine, and has a killer Web site with lots of free stuff and some you have to pay for, which is well worth it.

Speaking Presentations

Story Theater (www.storytheater.net). Public speaking is vital in creating and breathing a brand. Whether it's for a corporate brand or your personal one, Doug Stevenson (www.dougstevenson.com) is the master "storytelling" coach. He has been teaching his unique method to deliver great presentations for years. He conducts workshops around the country, has released a wonderful new book (*Never Be Boring Again*), and offers lots of free resources on his Web site. If you do any public speaking and care about your brand, check out Stevenson's offerings.

Trends

Trendscape: Tracking the Future of Cool (www.trendsetters.com). Trendsetters.com is a San Francisco–based media and entertainment company that provides services aimed at reaching trendsetters globally. Trend analyst and founder Michael Tchong is an internationally recognized trend expert and successful entrepreneur. In addition to writing a free trendsetter online newsletter, Tchong consults and speaks on emerging market trends and consumer buying issues.

Visual Merchandising

Visual Merchandising Trade Association (www.vmta.org). Dedicated to raising the profile of the visual merchandising profession within the retail community while promoting its services and its strategic role, the VMTA Web site has good articles and allows you to post talent needs. A professional membership provides an array of other valuable services.

Recommended Reading

Here are a few of my favorite books on branding and business.

Abrams, Bill. *The Observational Research Handbook: Understanding How Consumers Live with Our Product.* New York: McGraw-Hill (formerly NTC Business Books), 2000.

Asacker, Tom. *Sandbox Wisdom.* Manchester, N.H.: Eastside Publishing, 2000.

Blasingame, Jim. *Small Business Is Like a Bunch of Bananas.* Florence, Ala.: SBN Books, 2002.

Blasingame, Jim. *$10,000 of Small Business Consulting—For the Price of This Book!* Florence, Ala.: SBN Books, 2003.

Dru, Jean-Marie. *Beyond Disruption.* New York: John Wiley & Sons, 2002.

Falk, Edgar A. *1001 Ideas to Create Retail Excitement.* New York: Prentice-Hall, 1994.

Francese, Peter. *Marketing Insights to Help Your Business Grow.* Ithaca, N.Y.: Paramount Market Publishing, 2002.

Gitomer, Jeffrey. *Customer Satisfaction Is Worthless, Customer Loyalty Is Priceless.* Atlanta: Bard Press, 1998.

Gitomer, Jeffrey H. *The Sales Bible.* New York: William Morrow and Company, Inc., 1994.

Glickman, David. *Punchline Your Bottom Line.* Tampa, Fla.: Keynote Comedy, 2003.

Godin, Seth. *Purple Cow.* SethGodin.com, 2002.

Gobé, Marc. *Emotional Branding: The New Paradigm for Connecting Brands to People.* New York: Allworth Press, 2001.

Griffin, Jill. *Customer Loyalty: How to Earn It, How to Keep It.* San Francisco: Jossey-Bass, 2002.

Griffin, Jill and Michael Lowenstein. *Customer Winback: How to Recapture Lost Customers and Keep Them Loyal.* San Francisco: Jossey-Bass, 2001.

Hill, Sam. *60 Trends in 60 Minutes.* New York: John Wiley & Sons, 2002.

Meyers, Herbert and Richard Gerstman. *Branding at the Digital Age.* New York: Interbrand/Palgrave, 2001.

Michalko, Michael. *Cracking Creativity: Secrets of Creative Genius.* Berkeley, Calif.: Ten Speed Press, 1991.

Michalko, Michael. *Thinkertoys: The Handbook of Business Creativity.* Berkeley, Calif.: Ten Speed Press, 1991.

Michalko, Michael. *Thinkpak: A Brainstorming Card Deck.* Berkeley, Calif.: Ten Speed Press, 1994.

Neumeier, Marty. *The Brand Gap.* Indianapolis: New Riders Publishing, 2003.

Salzman, Marian, Ira Matathia, and Ann O'Reilly. *Buzz: Harness the Power of Influence and Create Demand.* New York: John Wiley & Sons, 2003.

Stevenson, Doug. *Never Be Boring Again.* Colorado Springs, Colo.: Cornelia Press, 2003.

Trout, Jack. *Differentiate or Die.* New York: John Wiley & Sons, 2002.

Underhill, Paco. *Why We Buy: The Science of Shopping.* New York: Simon & Schuster, 1999.

Index

About the Author

Since February 12, 1960, Karen Post has been developing creative solutions and implementing innovative methods that cause action. Just ask her mom.

In 1982, at the age of twenty-two, Karen began building memorable brands that sold products, moved audiences, persuaded public opinion, captured votes, and calmed unrest. She has organized and led three successful companies—an ad agency for eighteen years, a litigation communications consulting firm, a consulting and speaking practice (the last two are still active), and a dot.com that she tries to forget.

Known as the Branding Diva, Karen is a passionate entrepreneur, national speaker, branding enthusiast, and consultant. She works with professionals and organizations to "Land Their Brands" by maximizing their impact through strategic distinction and effective communications.

Karen is the monthly branding contributor to fastcompany.com. She has been featured in print, broadcast, and online media, and her writings are regularly published in the United States and abroad.

Karen's talents have benefited many businesses, from emerging start-ups to Fortune 500 organizations, including for-profit companies, non-profit associations, industry leaders, athletic professionals, and elected officials.

When Karen's not working, which is rare, you will find her on a tennis court, at the movies, or eating sushi at Samurai Blue.